*Praise for **Modus Operandi: A Writer's Guide to How Criminals Work,** also by Mauro V. Corvasce and Joseph R. Paglino*

"Read [*Modus Operandi*] and learn exactly how bad guys hot-wire stolen cars, break into impregnable-looking safes and make homicides look like accidents." —*The Washington Post*

"It's all well organized, and concise, but not so detailed that budding lawbreakers could use it as instructional. Even if you don't aspire to be the next Dick Francis, this is fascinating reading. If you do see your name on the title page of a crime novel, it's essential." —*Booklist*

"Professional writers will find it a handy reference text, and members of the public who are hooked on television police shows will have a new armchair guide." —*The Dallas Morning News*

"Provides information on everything from Arsonists to White-collar Crime and Money Laundering—and how the criminals were caught." —*P.I. Magazine*

*Praise for the **Howdunit Writing Series:***

"Read the entire 'Howdunit' series—including *Deadly Doses* and *Armed & Dangerous*—and embarking on a life of crime seems a definite possibility." —*The Washington Post*

"Essential buys for any serious author . . . will cut research time in half!" —*Mystery Scene Magazine*

"Chock full of fantastic information, incredibly entertaining and highly recommended. If you don't have these books, run (don't walk!) to your nearest bookseller and order the entire series." —*The Gila Queen's Guide to Markets*

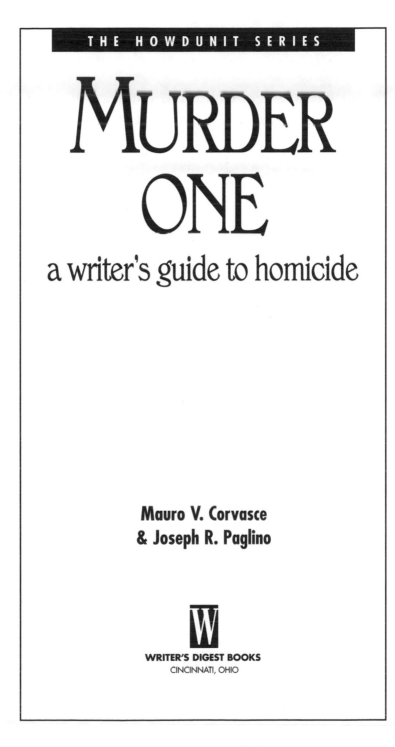

THE HOWDUNIT SERIES

MURDER ONE

a writer's guide to homicide

**Mauro V. Corvasce
& Joseph R. Paglino**

WRITER'S DIGEST BOOKS
CINCINNATI, OHIO

Dedication

To our wives, Elizabeth and Michelle, and to our children—Kristina and Nicholas, Christopher and Danielle.

Murder One: A Writer's Guide to Homicide. Copyright © 1997 by Mauro V. Corvasce and Joseph R. Paglino. Printed and bound in the United States of America. All rights reserved. No part of this book may be reproduced in any form or by any electronic or mechanical means including information storage and retrieval systems without permission in writing from the publisher, except by a reviewer, who may quote brief passages in a review. Published by Writer's Digest Books, an imprint of F&W Publications, Inc., 1507 Dana Ave., Cincinnati, Ohio 45207. (800) 289-0963. First edition.

Other fine Writer's Digest Books are available from your local bookstore or direct from the publisher.

01   00   99   98   97   5   4   3   2   1

Library of Congress Cataloging-in-Publication Data

Corvasce, Mauro V.
    Murder one: a writer's guide to homicide / by Mauro V. Corvasce, Joseph R. Paglino.—1st. ed.
        p.   cm.
    Includes index.
    ISBN 0-89879-773-X (alk. paper)
    1. Detective and mystery stories—Authorship. 2. Crime writing—Authorship. 3. Crime—Research. I. Paglino, Joseph R. II. Title.
PN3377.5.D4C674   1997
808.3'872—dc21   97-26703
                                                                             CIP

Content edited by Jack Heffron
Production edited by Patrick G. Souhan
Cover illustration by Chris Spollen

Acknowledgment

I would like to thank my wife, Elizabeth, and my children, Kristina and Nicholas. Also, for their help in making this book a reality, I thank all the wonderful people at Writer's Digest Books, especially William Brohaugh, Jack Heffron and Stacie Berger. A nod of thanks goes to our agent Steven Axelrod for his continuous support and assistance, and also to all the extraordinary writers we have met throughout the country while lecturing at conferences. Finally, a thanks to Joseph, for continuous admiration and friendship on future endeavors.

Mauro V. Corvasce

First and foremost, I would like to thank my wonderful wife, Michelle, who has been my rock, my great listener, my advisor, but most important of all, my very best friend. She has always believed in me and put up with the long hours dedicated to this project, in addition to the rigors of detective work.

I would also like to thank my two wonderful children, Christopher and Danielle, for understanding that Daddy had a lot of work to do on this project, that he loves them, and that he would always make their hockey, baseball and soccer games in spite of the rough schedule.

To my mom, "Ginger," for keeping our family together during tough times and making sure I went to the best schools she could afford, even if it meant she did without. I don't know where I would be today without her.

To William Brohaugh, Jack Heffron and the great people at Writer's Digest Books for their confidence in us and their continued support.

To all the friends who supported me and gave me encouragement to go on. Their sincere thoughts and kind words will never be forgotten.

To Mr. Anthony Robbins, who has motivated me to always reach for the stars, believe in myself and never quit. His positive outlook on life, family and success were a godsend to me during the last four years.

Last but not least, to all the fellow police officers who are entrusted with the investigation of the planet's most serious crime—murder. Their tireless hours dedicated to solving these crimes is surely not forgotten by the wives, husbands, brothers, sisters, mothers, fathers and children of the victims.

Joseph R. Paglino

About the Authors

Mauro V. Corvasce and Joseph R. Paglino are detectives with the Monmouth County Prosecutor's Office in New Jersey. They have more than thirty-five years combined experience in law enforcement. They collaborated on another book in the Howdunit series titled *Modus Operandi: A Writer's Guide to How Criminals Work*, and they speak frequently at writer's conferences. They have appeared together on numerous television and radio programs, including CNN's "ShowBiz Today," National Public Radio's "All Things Considered," and "Good Day, New York."

Mauro V. Corvasce is the supervisor of Major Crimes Investigation Unit and Identification Bureau in Monmouth County. He began his career as a patrol officer, and has worked in the following departments: Juvenile, Sex Crimes/Child Abuse, Arson, Narcotics and Forensics. He now investigates homicides. He is certified as a crime scene analyst, a polygraphist and fingerprint analyst. He has lectured at the Federal Bureau of Investigation Academy, Naval Criminal Investigative Service, Monmouth County Police Academy, Monmouth University and Brookdale Community College. He holds twenty-eight Letters of Commendation for excellence in police work and has been selected Police Officer of the Year in Monmouth County.

Joseph R. Paglino holds a Master's Degree in Forensic Psychology and is pursuing a Ph.D. in Psychology. He has taught fingerprint analysis, photography, crime scene investigation and Spanish at police academies and universities, and he is an instructor for the National Sheriffs Association. As a detective in New Jersey and in Brooklyn, New York, he has worked in the following departments: White Collar Crime, Sex Crimes/Child Abuse, Bureau of Technical and Forensic Services, Major Offense/Career Criminal, Transit Crime, Auto Crime, the Supreme Court Bureau and the Night Fugitive Strike Force. His participation in an undercover "sting" operation earned him the President's Award for Outstanding Police Service in 1992.

Table of Contents

Introduction

Every day of our lives we read about or hear about murder. We see it on the nightly news. We watch movies and TV shows about murder. We read about it in novels and true-crime books. From street gang drive-by shootings to husbands killing their wives to strangers killing strangers for seemingly insignificant reasons, we witness the world of murder every day from the safety of our living rooms. And yet the topic never fails to interest us.

The reason for this fascination, we believe, is because murder is the most horrible crime a human being can commit. A life has been taken. A human being—along with all of that person's beliefs and memories, emotions and desires, thoughts and ideas—has been killed. Murder is, therefore, an act against humanity itself. It strikes a basic, primal chord in all of us. Writers like you continue to explore the subject of murder because of this.

In this book, we will not presume to tell you how to write about murder. You already know how to create vivid characters, how to describe settings so your readers feel they are right there, how to build plots that keep those readers turning the pages. Our talents and knowledge are not in telling stories. We solve crimes. Between us, we have more than thirty-five years of criminal investigative experience. During that time, we have investigated a great many murders, and seen a great many things we would just as soon not have seen.

But through this book, we can use our experience to help you write more accurately about how—and why—murders occur. We have tried to make *Murder One* an encyclopedia of murder, covering all the common types of murder writers use in stories, novels, scripts, screenplays and true-crime books. Our goal is to help you get the facts right. Writers have told us that our earlier book, *Modus Operandi: A Writer's Guide to How Criminals Work*, and other books in the Howdunit series also help them get ideas for their novels. If a particular case or detail in this book sparks an idea in your imagination, that's great. But we'll leave the creative stuff to you.

Over the years, we've seen too many stories go wrong because a writer makes a key technical mistake. Or a lot of little mistakes. Or the entire fictional world of crime, criminals and police just doesn't ring true. This book will show you how murders are committed in the real world. In each chapter, we'll give you the following:

- an overview of the type of murder under discussion

- common motives for each type of murder

- common methods used in each type of murder

- common techniques used in investigating and solving each type of murder

We'll also give you examples from cases we've worked on or are familiar with to give you a clearer sense of how real-life murders take place. Every murder, of course, has unique aspects to it, so in some chapters, we've created fictional scenarios that represent in a general way how the type of murder under discussion usually occurs. Finally, we'll offer brief "tips" focusing on some small details that too often writers get wrong.

While writing *Murder One*, we've kept in mind the questions we usually hear when we speak at writers conferences, and we have tried to answer them. We've focused on the subjects we felt would most interest you (and be of most use to you) as a writer. This book is not designed as a police training manual. It's designed for writers.

One warning: The world of murder investigation is not a pretty one. It's definitely not for the squeamish or the faint of heart. Though we have avoided including gratuitously grisly details, we do want to present a candid, accurate picture of how murderers think and act. So some of the descriptions are harsh. Read at your own risk.

The investigation of murder is not an exact science. Every case, every killer, is a little different. Solving a case sometimes involves intuition, accident or just a lucky break. But murders do fall into certain categories, murderers do share certain traits and motives, and investigative techniques do exist for gathering and analyzing clues. We'll share these with you.

With the facts you'll find in this book, you will create stories that are more accurate and more detailed. And you will be able to probe more deeply into this subject that fascinates us all—the act of murder.

O N E

AN OVERVIEW
OF MURDER

In this book, we will discuss a wide variety of murders. Sexual and serial murders. Contract murders. Vehicular murders. And many others. Though some of these types of murders are similar in certain ways, each is unique in its motivations and its methods. If, for example, your murderer is motivated by lust, his methods of killing will be much different from those of the character who is motivated by a need for narcotics.

But before we can talk about all the different types of murder, we must know exactly just what a murder is. Although actual laws and mitigating factors will vary by state, the crime of killing another human being is considered the most serious offense throughout the United States. That fact is proven by its carrying the most serious penalty the courts can pass—death.

The Legal Terms

The following terms are taken from the New Jersey State Law Code of Criminal Justice. The definitions may vary slightly from state to state, so be sure you check the state code of criminal justice in whichever state your fiction is set. These definitions, however, are fairly standard, and it is unlikely your own state will vary too much from them.

Criminal Homicide: A person is guilty of criminal homicide "if he purposely, knowingly, recklessly . . . causes the death of another human being. Criminal homicide is murder, manslaughter, or death by auto."

Death by Auto or Vessel: "[occurs when death] is caused by driving a vehicle or vessel recklessly."

Manslaughter: "[occurs when the] actor recklessly causes death under circumstances manifesting extreme indifference to human life."

Murder: "[occurs when the] actor purposely [or knowingly] causes death or serious bodily injury resulting in death."

Self-Defense: "[is] the use of force upon or toward another . . . when the actor reasonably believes that such force is immediately necessary for the purpose of protecting himself against the use of unlawful force by such other person on the present occasion."

Homicide Investigations

In the chapters on particular types of murders, we explain how investigations are conducted for each type. But all homicide investigations follow a basic procedure, which we have outlined below. Before we get into it, however, you need to keep a couple of facts in mind. First, most homicides that get solved are done so within the first forty-eight hours. After that period of time, the trail generally runs cold. This is true for several obvious reasons:

1. Eyewitnesses who have not stepped forward probably will not appear. And their memories of the event, of course, become less clear.

2. New clues at the scene of the crime probably will not surface after the initial investigation and analysis have been completed.

3. If the murderer has left a trail of clues or if the police

know where the killer is hiding, an arrest has been made or is imminent.

Secondly, because the first forty-eight-hour period is so important, detectives work around the clock to gather evidence and follow up leads. Throughout the investigation, the homicide squad from the county prosecutor's office lends full assistance.

Finally, in most homicides, the victim knew the killer. For this reason, investigators focus their attention on the victim's immediate circle of family, friends and co-workers. Clues and motives are analyzed with this circle of people in mind. In the chapter on stranger and familiar stranger murders, you'll learn that these murders are very difficult to solve because the killer is not part of this circle. Investigators have no shortlist of likely suspects to keep in mind while analyzing the facts of the crime.

Step 1. Secure the Scene

The responsibility of the first officer at the scene of a crime is to preserve its integrity until the patrol supervisor can arrive. The officer should not move any objects or bodies and should keep bystanders from intruding on the scene. The supervisor— a sergeant or lieutenant—must ensure that the crime scene is preserved. Responsibilities of patrol officers include these tasks:

- surrounding the area with police tape

- controlling crowds

- preventing overzealous members of the media or family members of the victim from destroying or removing crucial evidence

Step 2. Find Eyewitnesses

Although eyewitness testimony is not always considered 100 percent accurate, finding such witnesses is the patrol officers' foremost duty once the crime scene is preserved and the patrol supervisors arrive on the scene. The officers however, do not interview these eyewitnesses themselves. They record the names and addresses of any people in the area and ask them to wait to speak with the homicide detectives when they arrive.

Step 3. Photograph the Crime Scene

When the detectives arrive, their first job is to photograph the crime scene. Their work is monitored by their own supervisors (who are detective sergeants or detective lieutenants) Several photos must be taken of the crime scene:

- shot from the four corners of the scene
- long-distance shots
- medium-distance shots
- close-up shots of the body and any evidence
- shots of any relevant details, selected by the detectives

Step 4. Search for Latent Prints

Fingerprinting at a crime scene is referred to by police officers as searching for latent prints. Police officers and detectives who are qualified should dust for prints. The following are among the most likely targets for fingerprinting:

- weapons
- points of entry or exit, such as doors and windows
- flat, hard surfaces such as tabletops

There are several different types of fingerprint powders used by the detectives, because a fingerprint might only show up when a certain type of powder is used. The most common types:

- black, for use on light objects
- white, for use on black items
- silver, for mirrors

As you surely know, no two persons' fingerprints are exactly alike. Also note that fingerprints do not come out clearly on porous material. To search for latent prints, the detectives use an ostrich feather fingerprint duster to apply the appropriate color powder to the area. They then, in a rapid, circular motion, twist the duster to spread the powder over the area. When a potential fingerprint is revealed by the powder, a special strip of tape is used to actually "lift" the fingerprint from the object. This tape is then examined by fingerprint experts and compared to prints stored on local, state and federal crime computers.

If you want to know more about fingerprinting, consult

the Howdunit titled *Scene of the Crime*, by Anne Wingate. She covers the topic in greater detail than we can offer here.

Step 5. Gather Evidence

Detectives can be looking for details as subtle as footprints or items as small as clothing fibers, hair strands, blood samples or paint chips. Such "trace evidence" is manipulated through tweezers and other instruments appropriate for dealing with objects of such minute size or substance. It is then transferred to a slide and sent to a forensics lab for examination.

Officers wear gloves when handling larger items, such as weapons, and deposit these items in plastic or paper bags. Whenever evidence is gathered, the name of the detective who found and returned it to the police station is carefully recorded. The name of the police officer who received it at the evidence locker at the local or county police station is also noted. This is called the chain of evidence and is used to ensure the reliability of evidence at trial.

Step 6. Remove the Body

By this stage in the investigation process, the county coroner has arrived. The coroner must make examinations of several key issues:

- the temperature
- the humidity
- the weather in the area

The coroner uses these notations in order to later establish the time of death to a greater degree of accuracy. The body is taken to the county morgue, where an autopsy is performed, revealing (usually) the cause of death.

To learn more about this process—and the next steps in determining cause of death—please consult the Howdunit titled *Cause of Death*, by Dr. Keith Wilson.

Under Arrest

A point before beginning: The following procedure for arresting a suspect does not apply only to murder cases. The same procedure is followed no matter what crime the suspect is alleged to have committed. If you have your detective follow this procedure in booking a murder suspect, you can be assured of its accuracy.

In order to arrest a suspect, the police must have "probable cause"; that is, there must be some substantive evidence linking the suspect to the alleged crime. Either immediately before or immediately after an arrest, the police in some jurisdictions must receive an arrest warrant from a judge, which will determine the initial amount of bail. This figure can later be changed at the formal bail hearing, which is usually within twenty-four hours.

Following an arrest, a variety of forms must be filled out to protect the suspect's constitutional rights, physical safety and personal property.

1. *Arrest Report.* This is one of the main forms to be completed. It contains details of the arrest, the bail amount, the suspect's name and information (address, date of birth, Social Security number, employer, address of employer, height, weight, eye color, scars, tattoos, color hair, etc.), and any other relevant facts pertaining to the case.

2. *Fingerprint Form.* This is another one of the major forms needed. Upon arrest, each suspect is fingerprinted three times: once for local police records, once for state police records, once for the FBI.

3. *Vehicle/Property Report.* Whenever the police impound a car or seize personal property during an arrest or as the result of a warranted search, they are required to fill out one of these forms to ensure the property can be returned if the suspect is found not guilty.

4. *Evidence Report Form.* Any evidence seized by the police during an arrest or a warranted search must also be cataloged on these forms, which are sent to the prosecutor. This helps with the efficient development of a case against the suspect.

5. *Suicide Evaluation Form.* During any interviews police officers have with the suspect, they observe her behavior. Based on what they notice, the police complete this form to estimate the probability of the suspect's attempting

suicide. If that is determined to be a distinct possibility, the police are required to post extra watch on the holding cell.

Writing Accurately About Murder

Before launching into weapons of murder and the specific types of murder, let us remind you that every murder has its own unique qualities. Though we have been investigating murders for many years, we always find something new or surprising. The following chapters will help you present your fictional murders in accurate ways, but be aware that there are exceptions to every rule.

Now, to close this chapter, let us offer you a few more facts about murder in America. The source of these statistics is a special report compiled by John M. Dawson for the Bureau of Justice Statistics, U.S. Department of Justice.

- More than half of all murder victims in large cities are young black males—who are killed by other young black males. The vast majority of the murderers, and even a large percentage of their victims, have had previous trouble with the law.

- While 48 percent of the general population is between the ages of fifteen and forty-five, 75 percent of the murder victims and 91 percent of defendants are in that age range.

- Seventy-five percent of murder victims and 90 percent of defendants are males.

- In large urban counties, circumstances involving illegal drugs account for 18 percent of the defendants and 16 percent of the victims.

- In large urban counties, handguns are used in 50 percent of the murders; knives are used in 21 percent of the murders.

- While 52 percent of the general population is female, only one in ten murder defendants and just over two in ten murder victims is female.

- A third of the female victims, but only one in ten male victims, are killed by their spouses or romantic partners.

- Six of every ten arrests for murder result in a murder conviction.
- More than 99 percent of defendants in capital offense cases—those with a murder charge that could result in a death penalty—are convicted of some charge.

WEAPONS OF MURDER

Every act of murder involves a weapon, such as a firearm, a knife or a blunt object. In certain types of murders, the weapon is the murderer's hands or other parts of his body, for example, his feet, if he has trained in martial arts or if he uses his feet to stomp a person to death. For the purpose of this chapter, we will not cover weapons that are part of the perpetrator's body.

Firearms

Since firearms are used in many of the types of murder we'll be discussing, we'll look at them first. The science by which a bullet, cartridge case or shotgun shell casing can be identified as having been fired by a particular weapon, to the exclusion of all other weapons, is known as ballistics. The caliber of a weapon, in general, denotes the nominal bore diameter of a barrel measured in either hundredths of an inch or in millimeters. This provides an initial grouping capability, such as referring to a weapon as a .22 caliber or a 9mm.

These designations expand from the basic caliber grouping in a variety of ways. Each denotes a specific cartridge case size and configuration. While some cartridges are interchangeable, most are specific for a weapon of a particular cartridge designation. Among some popular caliber designations are the following:

- descriptive words, such as .38 Special, .41 Magnum, .380 Auto or 9mm Corto

- manufacturer's or designer's name, such as a .30 Remington, 6mm Remington or .257 Roberts

When bullets or cartridges are compared by ballistics experts to see if they are fired from a particular weapon, they are looking for the general rifling characteristics of that weapon, such as the number of lands and grooves, the dimensions, the direction of the twist and rifling, and the caliber. Some types of examinations on bullets are done to look for the marks on the bullets that can be produced by rifling (the spinning around in the barrel as the bullet discharges from the weapon) or possibly by loading the weapon. Markings on the fired cartridge case or shotgun shell casing can be produced by any of the following parts of the weapon:

- breech face—the area the round is pushed through before it is seated and in position to be struck by the firing pin

- firing pin—a nail-shaped pin that rests behind the cartridge

- chamber—the area where the bullet rests prior to firing

- extractor—a small piece of metal inside the chamber that hooks into the shell casing as the bullet is being fired

- ejector—a small, square piece of metal with a spring that pushes the shell case out of the chamber

Unfired cartridges or shotgun shells are also important evidence at a murder scene. The ballistics expert needs to determine whether they were simply not shot through the weapon; the weapon misfired, causing the murderer to resort to a second weapon; or the cartridges or shotgun shells were, in fact, never even used. It is possible to determine whether the unfired cartridge or shotgun shell was loaded into and extracted from a weapon by noting the presence or lack of extractor and/or ejector marks on the bullet.

Let's go over some terminology that is useful for understanding firearms and depicting them accurately in your work.

Assault rifle: A fully automatic weapon that fires an intermediate cartridge, which is larger than a pistol cartridge but smaller than a full-size rifle cartridge. Assault rifles are normally selective fire and fed by a detachable magazine.

Autoloading: A firearm action in which the propellant gases or recoiling forces traded by the firing cartridge are used to open and close the mechanism of a firearm. The autoloading mechanism extracts each fired case from the chamber, ejects the spent case from the firearm and then chambers a loaded cartridge in preparation for the next shot.

Automatic (fully automatic): An autoloading action that will fire a succession of cartridges, as long as the trigger is depressed or until the ammunition supply is exhausted. Automatic weapons are machine guns subject to the provisions of the BATF. The term "automatic" is often incorrectly applied to semiautomatic rifles, pistols and weapons.

Caliber: A term used to describe ammunition. Caliber is the approximate diameter of a projectile. In the United States, caliber is usually written in inches, such as .30 caliber. In most other countries of the world, caliber is usually written in millimeters, such as 7.62mm.

When describing ammunition, you must be specific; cite more than just the diameter of the projectile, as there are, for example, many different .30 caliber cartridges. Therefore, additional information is used to describe specific ammunition. Unfortunately, there is no standard system for describing this ammunition. In the United States, a specific cartridge may be described by its caliber plus the year of its introduction, such as .30 caliber/06; the caliber plus the name of the weapon for which it was designed, as in .30 Carbine; the caliber plus the name of the designer, for example, .30 caliber Newton; and so forth. Most other countries identify ammunition by its diameter plus the length of the cartridge, such as 7.62 × 63mm.

There are many other terms that are used to further describe specific ammunition.

Double-action: A type of operation normally associated with revolvers, where pulling the trigger rotates the cylinder, cocks and fires the weapon. This term is also used to describe certain semi-automatic pistols where pulling the trigger will cock and fire the first shot.

Handgun: A weapon originally designed, made and intended to fire a small projectile (bullet) from the barrel, when held in one hand, and having a short stock (grip), designed to be gripped by one hand and at an angle to, and extending below, the line of the bore.

Machine gun: Any weapon that, by a single function of the trigger, shoots, is designed to shoot or can be readily restored to shoot automatically more than one shot without manual reloading.

Pistol: Any handgun that does not contain its ammunition in a revolving cylinder. Pistols may be single-shot, manually operated repeaters, semiautomatic or fully automatic.

Revolver: A handgun that contains its ammunition in a revolving cylinder. The Saturday Night Special fits into this category.

Rocket launcher: A device for launching a rocket-propelled projectile usually having a high-explosive warhead. Weapons of this type are designed to be used against armored vehicles in fortified positions. The ammunition for rocket launchers is usually also a destructive device.

Semiautomatic: Any autoloading action that will fire only a single shot for each single function of the trigger.

Serial numbers: Current regulations require that the serial number of a firearm must be conspicuously located on the frame or receiver. Common serial number locations include the side of the frame, on the butt, under the crane (yoke) or on the front strap.

Single-action: A type of operation normally associated with revolvers where the hammer must be manually cocked for each shot. The manual cock also rotates the cylinder, bringing another cartridge in line with the barrel for firing. The term is also used to describe certain semiautomatic pistols that must be manually cocked prior to firing the first shot.

Submachine gun: A simple, fully automatic weapon that fires a pistol cartridge. Submachine guns are also referred to as machine pistols.

Trigger pull: The amount of pressure necessary to fire a weapon. This pressure is normally used to measure whether a weapon was fired accidentally or on purpose. Trigger pull can be adjusted after market by an experienced gunsmith, so the trigger pull that is found on a weapon at a scene may not be the actual trigger pull with which the weapon was originally designed.

An example of this is a weapon with a hair trigger, so called because it doesn't take much trigger pull or pressure for the weapon to go off. A hair trigger allows a bullet to be quickly rechambered so the gun can be shot more rapidly.

One of the most common mistakes we have seen by authors in describing firearms is the use of the word *clip* to describe the holder that contains bullets in an automatic or semi-automatic weapon. There is no such thing as a clip in a semiautomatic or automatic weapon. It is in reality called a magazine.

Revolvers vs. Automatic and Semiautomatic Pistols

Additionally, one must remember the basic differences between a revolver and an automatic or semiautomatic weapon. In a revolver, the casing or shell from the spent bullet does not eject automatically, but can be ejected manually by activating the cylinder release, opening the cylinder so all casings are visible and dumping the shell casings on the ground. In an automatic weapon, of course, these ejections are, well, automatic.

Reloading revolvers is very time-consuming, so manufacturers produce what are known as speed loaders. These are round cylinders that have the five or six bullets already in them. When the casings have been emptied from a weapon that has been fully discharged, the speed loader lines up with the holes, and by pushing a small rod, the speed loader automatically pushes the new bullets in line with the cylinder of the revolver.

Revolvers

If we were looking at a revolver on the table with the butt or grip on the right-hand side and the front sight or barrel on the left-hand side, we would describe it in the following manner: The small metal notch on the barrel of the weapon is called the front sight. If we were to proceed along the top of the barrel and work our way back toward the hammer or the actual lever that gets cocked to fire the weapon, the rear sight would be just before the hammer on the same plane. The front sight (a small mark) and the rear sight (a U-shaped piece of metal) should be aligned perfectly on the target before a weapon is fired. This is known as the sight picture.

The revolving part of the revolver, in which bullets are loaded, is called the cylinder. Depending on the manufacturer, the cylinder will rotate either clockwise or counterclockwise. Cylinders carry five or six rounds. Police officers must know which way the cylinder rotates in case they have to reload the weapon during a "combat" situation, in which they are under assault from another person with a firearm.

TIP

In cases where we have seen persons play Russian roulette, revolvers were always used because only revolvers can leave some rounds not in the chamber, thus keeping you guessing until you pull the trigger. With an automatic or semiautomatic, the bullets are in a magazine and are automatically force-fed each time you pull the trigger. The pistol therefore will continue to fire every time the trigger is pulled until the magazine is empty.

The trigger on a revolver is pulled to produce the fired shot. The rounded area of metal around the trigger is called the trigger guard. The handle of the gun is called the grip, with the very bottom of the grip being called the butt. The cylinder release, which is the switch that allows the cylinder to fall sideways out of the gun so the spent casings can be released, is usually located between the cylinder and the grip. On most revolvers, the grips are made of wood but can be replaced with special rubber grips. The most commonly purchased brand of these rubber grips is produced by the Pachmayer company, known by cops as "packmayers." Some of these revolvers also have the serial numbers located inside the frame, and the grips must be removed in order to obtain the serial numbers.

Right above the cylinder on the main frame of the weapon is the top strap. In looking at the butt area of the weapon, the part to the immediate left of it, the front part of the grip, is called the front strap, and the rear of it, where the palm of the hand rests if the gun is gripped, is called the back strap.

Finally, the main component of the weapon, when all other parts have been disassembled, is called the frame. The frame and the remainder of the weapon (excluding the grips) are what is called stainless—blue or nickel—which refers to the finish placed on the weapon. Stainless may be of a bright or satin finish, and a blue finish is very dark (almost navy blue) and generally used by police officers so it won't be detected during undercover work or reflect light in the evening.

Semiautomatic Weapons

Looking at a conventional semiautomatic pistol placed on a table, we'd see the grip on the left-hand side with the barrel facing the right-hand side. The chamber is the part from which the shell casing is ejected when the pistol is fired. As with a revolver, there is a trigger and a trigger guard, and the front and rear straps are the same. The frame is also basically the same as that of the revolver. However, one major difference on the semiautomatic pistol is that there is a slide and ejection port and an extractor. The extractor is what makes the spent casing actually eject from the weapon. On most semiautomatics, the ejection port, if we were looking straight at the gun now on the table, is located dead center in the middle of the slide. The slide is the upper part of the semiautomatic pistol and runs from the rear of the gun all the way to the barrel. This slide is just like what it sounds: It slides back and forth every time the weapon is firing. Going back, the extractor rod pushes out the spent shell through the ejection port.

The other major difference between the semiautomatic and the revolver is that the semiautomatic's magazine or cartridge, which holds the bullets that are force-fed up into the gun as it

TIP

With most semiautomatic weapons, since they eject to the right, the spent shells land to the right of the people firing them. This is an important fact when writing because an experienced crime scene detective looks for the spent shells and casings from the semiautomatic pistol and places the shooter approximately two to three feet to the left of the shells.

is being fired, has a magazine release. When you press the magazine release on these weapons, you are disengaging the magazine from the rest of the weapon. Some manufacturers have their weapons designed so that when the magazine is released from the rest of the weapon, the pistol will not fire. Others will allow the pistol to fire, but there will only be one round left in it—the one that is chambered, all ready to go without being part of the magazine.

So, for example, if a semiautomatic pistol is rated as carrying fourteen shots, a person loads the magazine with only thirteen, slides the slide back and lets go quickly to chamber a round into position. Then she releases the magazine, which now only holds twelve, and replenishes it with the one that has moved up into the ejection area. Now the weapon is fully loaded with fourteen rounds ready to fire—one chambered and thirteen in the magazine.

Shotguns and Rifles

On shotguns and rifles, the thick area that's placed against the shooter's shoulder is called the stock. Some weapons have what is known as a recoil pad, or a thick rubber pad, at the very end of the butt of the stock to soften the blow to the shoulder. In the case of the double-barrel shotgun, there are two actual barrels: One is called an over-barrel and the other is called an under-barrel. This weapon is "broken open" when the top lever allows you to break the gun in half on a hinge and load the shells right into the chambers. The area underneath the barrels, where the hand is placed, is called the fore end. The receiver is where the shotgun shells are placed.

A bolt-action rifle has a front sight and a rear sight. The long barrel of the gun ends at a tip called the muzzle, and in some instances, the rear sight is also mounted at the rear of the barrel closest to the person firing the weapon. This weapon also has a trigger and trigger guard, with a device called a safety for locking the trigger so the weapon cannot be fired accidentally. The safety is usually located near the rear end of the bolt.

Pump-action or slide-action shotguns allow you to chamber a round after each one is fired and move it up from the magazine so it's ready to go. The difference between the pump action and the slide action (or lever action) and auto action of the weapons is that the autoloading of the slide action will continually move the shotgun shell into position without having to pump the weapon in order to prepare the next round. There can be minor differences in the nomenclature, but their purposes are basically the same.

Sharp Instruments

Any type of sharp instrument can be used to commit murder—scissors, knives, ice picks, metal combs, pitchforks, fireplace pokers, to name a few. We personally investigated a murder where the weapon was a set of knitting needles. They were jabbed into the eyes of an unfaithful husband while he slept.

Knives

The type of knife most often used to commit murder is the common household knife. This is because it is the most easily accessible knife to most people. Some examples of common household knives are place-setting knives, steak knives, carving knives and full-size butcher knives. Although many detective novels portray a switchblade or specialty knife being used, experience tells us that murderers use the simplest knives they can find.

Occasionally, specialty knives, such as the ninja knife, are used in murders. The ninja knife usually has a small blade (three to four inches long) and a large, curved handle. The murderer holds the knife with a full grip (like gripping a phone receiver) with the blade protruding between the middle and ring finger, and thrusts the knife in a punching motion so the blade sticks into and severs the victim's organs. If the knife is twisted or pulled down in the course of this punching motion, the victim's flesh is ripped open.

TIP

Ninja knives are commonly used by gangs when they can "get the drop," or sneak up, on the victims, who will simply think they are about to be punched. We have investigated many murder scenes in which bystanders had seen two people fighting and watched the winner walk away. Friends of the victims went to see if they were all right after the fights; upon rolling the bodies over, however, victims were found to have been stabbed many times with ninja knives.

A switchblade can be flicked open with a twist of the wrist or held in the closed position for the purpose of hiding the blade and then used by activating the lever to pop open the blade. As we mentioned earlier, switchblades are not often used in murders, as the blade support is not strong and has the potential to malfunction, causing the blade to fold back and cut off the fingers of the person using it.

An important component of a knife is called the hilt, which is where the handle meets the knife blade. If a person is stabbed with the hilt pressing up against the skin, there is a distinct discoloration of the skin, proving that the person who did the attacking was not simply defending himself but purposely pushing the knife blade in as far as it could go in an attempt to kill someone.

The double-edged knife is particularly deadly, having a sharp blade on both sides. This knife is used by professional or contract murderers, since it produces immediate and lethal results. Once the knife is pushed in, it doesn't matter whether the murderer moves it up or down; either way will produce severe cuts and perforation of the major organs of the body.

Unusual Weapons

In murders not committed with firearms, the perpetrators generally resort to using common household items as weapons, such as a fireplace poker or a frankfurter-style barbecue tool with a small pitchfork area. We have also seen cases where murder was committed using the following items: baseball bats, floor lamps, small televisions, VCRs, old-style metal telephones, chairs, typewriters, pots and pans, irons, cinder blocks and two-by-fours.

While these weapons are such common items they need not be described, we must remember that each one leaves trace evidence at the scene that can be collected by an experienced crime scene detective and matched to the weapon. Quite often in these types of cases, the murderer removes the weapon from the crime scene to avoid detection. Usually, however, in cases of crime-of-passion murders or murders that occur so spontaneously there is no time to plan the murder or cover it up, these weapons will be left at the scene. For this reason, an experienced detective will not assume a knife or other common household object left at a scene is a murder weapon brought in from the outside. On the other hand, some murderers have made the actual murder weapon appear to be from the victim's home.

In one case we investigated, a kitchen knife was brought to the scene by the murderer. After using it, he subsequently washed it off and placed it back in a knife block located on the kitchen counter. Detectives arriving on the scene had found the weapon in the knife block and determined that it was used, based on blood analysis at the scene of the murder.

Upon full analysis of the other knives and with the murder weapon also submitted to the state lab, it was positively determined that this weapon was in fact not the same knife that was usually found in the woman's home, but was brought in from the outside by the murderer. The murderer did not want the detectives to realize the knife may have been from his own home. Since this breakthrough in the investigation was kept out of the newspapers and because the murderer was content with the fact that the original press had noted the murder weapon was from the woman's own kitchen, the murderer neglected to throw out the rest of his knives.

Good old-fashioned detective work and a few lucky breaks resulted in the murderer being arrested with the remainder of his knives and knife block intact on his kitchen counter. This was crucial evidence because the murderer said he killed the victim in self-defense, picking up a knife from the victim's knife block simply to defend himself.

T H R E E

BUSINESS AND
FINANCIAL MURDERS

In a business or financial murder, the victim is killed for financial gain. This is not to be confused with an organized crime
group killing a person for money, which is covered in the chapter
on organized crime murders.

There are many reasons why someone would kill for financial gain. Take the businesswoman who, because of her greed,
attempts to take control of her partner's share of the business.
When she is unsuccessful, she comes to believe that the only
alternative is to kill her partner.

Competition among businesses is fierce and, in some circumstances, deadly. When one company or, shall we say, the
owner of a company, feels he is losing a share of his profits to
a competitor, he may believe the only way out is to eliminate
the competition. Another example of why one may kill to gain
control over a business or the company's assets is when one
partner discovers that another partner has been stealing from

the company. In this situation, the dishonest partner has two possible motives to kill:

1. to prevent the partner from advising the police

2. to kill the honest partner and blame her for the company's losses

Murder over money also occurs outside the realm of business. For example, when burglars, especially teenagers, are surprised by the homeowners' return during the burglary, they may kill them. There are two reasons why these teenagers would commit this type of murder:

1. They are inexperienced and therefore are more afraid of getting caught.

2. They usually burglarize homes in their own neighborhoods and can be recognized by their victims.

Financial murder can also occur when a person has a criminal past that is uncovered, usually by a co-worker. To keep her job, the criminal, ex-criminal, feels she must silence the person who knows about her past. Or perhaps the criminal is undertaking illegal activities through her job and, when discovered, must silence the co-worker to avoid detection.

Scenario: Bumping Off the Business Partner

Let's say there are two men who share equal rights in a company that manufactures gaskets for oil filters. The company is doing well, but not well enough for both partners to live a lavish life-style. The senior partner is in the midst of his midlife crisis and hooks up with a young woman who loves to spend his money. The wife of the senior partner becomes suspicious because her husband is spending a lot more money than usual.

Hence, the senior partner is becoming unraveled for two reasons: his newfound love and the fear that when his wife finds out, she'll take him to the cleaners. What is the senior partner to do?

Motives

Panic, fear and greed seem to be the greatest motives to kill. The senior partner in this scenario has developed all three. He determines that the best way to rectify the situation is to "rub out" his partner to gain control of the money.

It is standard procedure for business partners to have life insurance coverage in which one partner is the beneficiary if the other partner should die. And it just so happens that this is the case for our partners.

Methods

The senior partner decides to make it appear as if his partner has become depressed to the point of being suicidal. His next step is to make the homicide look like a suicide. This is a difficult task. Experienced detectives, forensic specialists and medical examiners have seen many such cases. But they are human and can make mistakes and oversights.

For example, the detective could be sent to the crime scene and misinterpret the manner of death. Since not all medical examiners respond to the scene, an autopsy would not be called for and undertaken. Instead, the victim's body simply would be shipped to the funeral parlor.

In our scenario, the senior partner comes up with a plan to make the employees think the junior partner is having personal problems. One method is to change business meetings to different locations and times without advising the junior partner so his absence is duly noted.

Another way to undermine the junior partner is to make it appear he is purchasing unnecessary equipment for the company. The senior partner continues with this sabotage until the employees think there is something seriously wrong with the junior partner. The senior partner may even ask the junior partner to seek medical and/or psychiatric help.

When the senior partner feels the time is right, he picks a time and a location to carry out his mission. In this case, the junior partner makes arrangements to come into the office on a Sunday morning to prepare the annual inventory. This is a practice the junior partner has been performing for many years, and it is well known by family, friends and company employees.

The senior partner also knows there will be no one else present at the business.

In the meantime, the senior partner has illegally purchased a weapon—most likely stolen and untraceable to him—from the seedy side of town and is seated at his desk "working" and waiting for his partner to arrive.

Keep in mind that there will be no sign of forced entry because the senior partner has the keys to the door. There will be no signs of a struggle between the two because the junior partner will not know until the very last moment what is about to happen. The senior partner only has to reach across the desk and shoot his partner somewhere in the head area, which is common in male suicides, and place the weapon in close proximity to the victim's body.

Investigation and Capture

In this case, the victim's fingerprints are not on the murder weapon, nor is there gunshot residue or trace metals on the body. This is determined by a gunshot residue examination, which is a forensic test in which the hands of the apparent shooter (the victim in this scenario) are wiped with a solution that is examined in a forensic laboratory for certain components of gunpowder. The other examination, commonly referred to as trace metal examination, is a test in which the hands are sprayed with a solution and examined under ultraviolet light in a darkened room. The purpose of this examination is to see the tracings of the metal where it came in contact with the person's skin. These examinations must be done within two to six hours after the shooting. We have never had a positive confirmation of gunpowder residue from a subject's hands, but we have read of them.

There are many reasons why the test so often turns up negative. One reason is the residue can easily be removed by hand washing. Also, when small-caliber ammunition is used, no residue presents itself to be analyzed.

A negative result in a trace metals examination is usually not as significant as it would be in other forensic examinations, since an absence of scientific evidence showing the weapon was placed in the hand of the victim does not mean the weapon wasn't placed in that hand. Many handguns today have frames made from plastic, wood or rubber, or a combination of the three, which renders the test useless. The trace metal examination is just a tool to help investigators provide the facts of the case—if a metal weapon was used.

Killing the Competition

When companies are in competition, there is always a winner and a loser, and the loser may sometimes perform dastardly deeds on the competition to eliminate them. One method would be to hire a person to kill the competition.

The business owner may choose from any number of potential "hitmen"—loyal friends or employees, or someone he is in daily contact with, such as a gas station attendant, mechanic, mail carrier, landscaper, pool attendant, country club valet or convenience store clerk. Regardless of whom the business owner chooses, the hired killer must be trustworthy and have the courage to take another's life.

Motives

People who agree to kill for money are typically low-paid workers who need cash. They are motivated by debt and need, as well as by greed. They will do anything to make money.

Other particularly strong motives for business/financial killings are love and family loyalty. The eldest son of a business owner, for example, may agree to kill the competition both out of family loyalty and desire for financial gain. The business owner tells his son that the family company, which has had continued success since Great-Great-Grandpa founded it back in the 1800s, is probably going to go out of business because of a rival company's newer, cheaper product.

Prejudice is another motive for this type of murder. In this scenario, you may have the owner of the company ask one of the managers to profile employees to determine a suitable candidate to become the killer. The business owner instructs the manager to tell her employee that he is in danger of losing his job because a competing company is hiring undocumented aliens to manufacture its cheaper products, which will force this employee's company out of business. The manager thereby preys on the employee's fears and prejudices to motivate him to accomplish the task at hand.

A final motive for a business/financial murder is desperation resulting from a major financial setback, such as medical expenses incurred by a sick wife or child or any other unexpected or urgent need for money.

Methods

To avoid detection, the murderer frequently disguises this type of murder by making it look like an unsuccessful robbery attempt. For example, if the owner of the competing business is working late one night, the murderer enters and shoots him and then ransacks the office, taking a few expensive items to make it look like a robbery.

In another scenario, the murder, on the surface, looks like an unsuccessful carjacking. One method of doing this: While driving, the murderer bumps the victim's vehicle, causing the victim to stop. The murderer jumps out and walks up to where the victim is still sitting in the driver's seat and shoots her. To ensure there are no witnesses, the murderer will have chosen a somewhat remote area. He would have watched the victim for days to track where the victim will probably be at a certain time.

Your best plan would be to have your victim get killed during the commission of another crime.

To get a better understanding of how criminals commit crime, read our first book, *Modus Operandi*. A cheap but necessary plug.

Covering Up a Bank Robbery

Someone may commit a crime for financial gain and then kill to cover up his involvement. The crime will have been carefully planned, and the victim will be someone who, for any number of reasons, uncovers the perpetrator's involvement in the crime.

If your character is going to rob a bank, he has been planning the robbery, in most cases, for quite a while. With the occasional crime of opportunity, however, a person just walks into the bank on the spur of the moment and robs it. Some of the conditions that can spark a crime of opportunity are a sudden or heavy snowfall or a power failure, because the suspect feels the opportunity is there for a quick in and a quick out. But remember, while this is happening, our suspect is not prepared. He may not have the simple necessities such as gloves, some type of mask and, of course, a weapon and the bag to hold the money. It is interesting to note that most bank robbers usually receive under five thousand dollars for all their hard work.

Motives

The motive for a bank robber to kill can be as simple as covering up the robbery. During the holdup, a police officer may be in the bank standing in line, waiting to do his own banking. He and the robber may recognize each other at the same moment, and the robber responds by shooting and killing the officer. Two motives are at work here:

1. the financial gain (why he is robbing the bank in the first place)
2. the cover-up of the robbery

In another situation, the robber may kill a bank guard who attempts to stop the robbery. A similar killing could take place in an armored car holdup in which the car attendants are killed. In this case, a customer trying to assist in apprehending the robber may even be shot.

In yet another scenario, the victim could be a customer who is shot because she poses some type of threat. Despite what is shown in some films and television shows, the typical threatening customer is the customer who is looking at the robber or is hysterical with fear. Most often this threat is caused not by heroism but by the customer's anxiety. The customer may begin yelling at the teller to hurry up. The customer's nervousness makes the robber nervous, so he kills the customer to gain a stronger sense of control over the situation.

Methods

The bank robber has plotted out all the details of the crime in advance. If he is an experienced criminal with a number of robberies under his belt, he expects certain things to happen during the robbery. When something out of the ordinary occurs, such as the off-duty police officer standing in line or the resistance of a security guard, he may feel compelled to use deadly force to attain his goal. Certain factors such as jail time and a criminal record or drug or alcohol abuse at the time of the robbery greatly impact the robber's behavior during the robbery. These factors increase the robber's fear of getting caught, and he is more likely to kill anyone who stands in her way.

In our experiences with robbery, robbers shot by the police or an armed guard flee, or even secure the situation by maintaining cover (guarding at gunpoint) on any potential threat. We have even had robbers get the money, only to drop it and flee.

Investigation and Capture

A common misconception about bank robberies is that the FBI is always called in because the money is guaranteed by government insurance. In actuality, the only time the FBI assists in an investigation is when either a weapon is used or a threat of using a weapon is made. Many robberies, therefore, are investigated by the local law enforcement agency.

Bank robberies are not especially difficult to investigate because of the number of witnesses involved. Armed guards and surveillance cameras also can provide descriptions of the robbers. Most bank robbers do rob a number of banks before being apprehended. When they *are* finally apprehended, it is usually because the police are notified and respond quickly while the robber is still in a bank or just exiting it. Again, the robber who has a prison record and will therefore receive a stiff sentence for the robbery is likely to try to shoot his way out, take hostages or kill whomever tries to stop him.

Case Study: Embezzlement

Consider this chain of events, which actually occurred: A man was working as the manager of a small business. He developed an expensive relationship with a young female employee. Over time, his money ran out and he began to use the company's capital. Knowing that the owner of the business would soon begin his yearly audit, the manager panicked and looked for ways to cover up the missing money. Finding none, he devised the following desperate plan.

He would purchase a gun off the street. When he felt the time was right (on an especially slow day at the business), he would rearrange the store so it looked like a robbery had occurred. Then he would use the gun to *kill* himself to make it appear as if he'd been murdered while protecting the company's money.

But he realized there would be many unanswered questions, such as why the weapon was still in the store, why there was gunshot residue on his hands and why the trace metals examination of the victim's hands would come out positive. The path of the bullet could also be determined as contact or close contact—all clues that would lead the police to determine it was a suicide.

So the dull-witted criminal secured an accomplice and slightly modified his original plan.

The store manager would shoot himself. When his accomplice heard the gunshot, he would enter the store, remove the gun, take the envelope of money that contained the start-up register money (as a fee for his services), walk to a pay phone and call 911.

When the manager did actually shoot himself, the accomplice walked in as planned, took the envelope with the money in it, removed the gun from the victim's hand, walked out the door and carefully placed the envelope and the gun in his pocket.

An employee at the business next door heard the gunshot and looked out the door to see a man exiting the neighboring business and putting the handgun in his pocket. The neighbor called the police and reported the incident and the description of the accomplice. While the accomplice made the 911 call, a patrol vehicle that just happened to be minutes away from the phone booth arrived on the scene and apprehended the 911 caller while he was still on the phone.

The accomplice looked as guilty as could be, and the police had his voice on the 911 call reporting the crime. They discovered the weapon used to shoot the victim in one pocket and the stolen cash in another.

The twist to this story is that the weapon was a small-caliber handgun, and instead of killing the intended victim, it severed his spinal cord, causing him to be paralyzed from the chest down. When the victim was finally able to talk to the police, he confessed everything to them. Remarkably, the owner of the business had tremendous sympathy for the manager and paid all of his medical expenses. When the man was able to return to work, he was given back his job

Avenging a Financial Loss

Let's look at the other side of the coin—when someone kills because money has been taken from him. This type of killing is usually done out of revenge and anger and may occur on the spur of the moment. Let's say a company manager discovers his employee has been stealing money over a period of time by inaccurately recording sales receipts. When the manager first makes the discovery, particularly if the victim happens to be close by, a verbal argument usually ensues. As the two exchange words and the argument becomes heated, a fight develops. The angry boss uses items at hand—a letter opener, a paperweight, perhaps a hammer—to injure, and eventually kill, the employee.

When the victim is discovered, his body will show definite signs of a struggle and may have many stab wounds or perhaps gunshot wounds (many gunshot wounds if a handgun was used). This brutality matches the boss's rage at the time of the assault.

TIP

The police use a procedure called bloodstain analysis, in which the bloodstain patterns are studied to determine the course of the assault and to recreate it. The examiner can determine the number of blows the victim suffered, the angle and force of the blows and whether the victim was standing when the blows occurred. When used accurately, this highly specialized discipline reconstructs the crime scene. This reconstruction is used to verify the victim's or witnesses' statements.

Once the assailant calms down, he may attempt to cover up the crime in a number of ways. He may call the police and report that it was self-defense or that upon returning to work, he discovered the victim's body.

In another cover-up attempt, the perpetrator may freeze the victim's body in a freezer, then dismember it. The frozen body will produce little or no blood. He may then place the body parts in several large plastic garbage bags, securing them tightly to prevent leakage when the body begins to thaw. These bags will then be thrown away in remote areas or thrown into a nearby river or lake.

We have discovered that these dumpings can occur at various times of the day. It depends on the perpetrator and his urgency to dispose of the body. We have also seen a number of cases where the perpetrator has driven around with the body in the trunk of his vehicle until he has located a suitable disposal area.

When there is preplanning involved in the murder, such factors as the location and method of disposing of the body will be taken into consideration, in addition to the murder itself. In the case of the wrathful manager and theiving employee, another scenario could be to bring the employee to a comfortable location so as to put him at ease. At some point, a heated discussion erupts over the circumstances and the boss shoots the victim. After the murder, the perpetrator may move the victim to an area such as a bathtub or a basement, where he will dissect the victim so the body can be transported more easily. The dissection is performed with a power saw, handsaw, axe, large butcher knife or any combination of the above. Again, the body will be neatly wrapped and transported to a remote location. It may or may not be buried, depending on location, time and the mental state of the perpetrator.

TIP

During a forensic examination, the tools used in a dismemberment (e.g., the blade of a power saw, hand saw, axe, large butcher knife or most other cutting implements) can be examined and a "mechanical fit" can be determined. The teeth of the saw can be matched to the cut area of the bone, just as a screwdriver can be identified as a tool used to pry open a door.

Scenario: Young Criminals

Motives and Methods

Teenagers and young adults (and, increasingly, children), though they may be only novice criminals, also kill to cover up crimes. Young people typically commit crimes of opportunity.

Let's say a group of children is playing ball in the street. They observe Mr. and Mrs. Jones, who are both dressed up, getting into their car and driving away. Young Johnny remembers that when he was helping Mrs. Jones clean up the garage, he saw Mr. Jones cleaning a handgun at the kitchen table. He also remembers that Mrs. Jones never locks the sliding glass door leading from the master bedroom, where the gun is kept, to the pool.

Johnny formulates a plan to enter the Joneses' residence to obtain Mr. Jones's handgun. The plan includes a lookout person who will watch from the street. The lookout will notify the person standing by the opened door of any approaching danger, and this person will pass the information on to Johnny, who will be in the house.

As the Joneses are en route to their destination, Mrs. Jones remembers she left something at home. The Joneses return home, and as Mrs. Jones gets out of the car, the street lookout leaves the area without giving warning, going against the plan.

Mrs. Jones enters the house through the front door, while one kid is standing at the rear of the house and another kid is searching the bedroom for the handgun. The perpetrator finds the gun at about the same time Mrs. Jones enters her bedroom. Startled by her unexpected entry, he turns and shoots her.

The kid who is standing outside hears the noise and enters the bedroom to see Mrs. Jones lying on the floor in a pool of blood. Knowing that Mr. Jones cannot be far behind, the pair could do one of two things: Flee the area prior to Mr. Jones's entry or wait for Mr. Jones to enter and kill him in an attempt to cover up their connection with the crime. (One thing is certain: The dialogue between the two juveniles is filled with stress and bewilderment, because at this point, they are so emotionally charged their actions will be controlled by their fears.)

By this time, Mr. Jones is becoming concerned about his

wife and decides to go in and look for her. As he enters the house, he calls out for her, which alerts the two thieves who are hiding and waiting. As Mr. Jones enters the bedroom, he sees his wife. He cries out to her while kneeling down, hoping it's not too late to render some assistance.

Mr. Jones doesn't know who shot his wife, and he is not aware of or fearful of any intruders or danger. As he is crouched over his wife, the young felon shoots Mr. Jones in the back with his own weapon.

At first, the two juveniles have a sense of curiosity and examine the two victims. In some cases, they may even perform some type of sexual act on Mrs. Jones, depending on the nature of her wounds and her appearance. While this is not a common occurrence, it *does* happen, usually with teenage boys going through puberty.

TIP

When juveniles rape and kill older, not-so-attractive ladies, they usually use some garment, towel or bag to cover the victims' face in an attempt to shield the murderers' eyes from what they perceive as being unattractive. When the victims are good-looking, our juveniles often perform a number of different procedures to appease their curiosity.

Now that the immediate danger of apprehension has passed, the two perpetrators search the house for additional valuables to steal, which will ultimately enable the police to connect them to the homicides of Mr. and Mrs. Jones. The Joneses' property may be found on the kids at some point, or if they sell the property in a pawnshop, the police can easily trace the evidence back to the pair. This is because in most jurisdictions, pawnshops must, by town ordinance, obtain written verification of the seller's identity prior to purchasing any item. A description of items along with the seller's identification must be maintained for at least a period of ninety days prior to the resale of any items bought.

The young killers become panic-stricken upon realizing that when the police do their investigation, they may find evidence at the scene that will link the two of them to the murder.

So they decide the best thing to do is to start a fire in an attempt to burn the Joneses' residence to the ground to cover up any evidence left at the scene.

To start this fire, the young felons must use material already available in the house. If there is an attached garage, they may find lawn mower gasoline, or they may use any other flammable liquid. If they do not use an accelerant, the fire will be slow-burning and easily spotted by neighbors. The slow-burning fires will do little or no damage to the bodies and the house.

In one case we remember, the perpetrator severely beat the victim and thought the blows to the victim's head had killed him. So in an attempt to cover up any evidence, the perpetrator decided to burn his victim's apartment. He piled clothing near to where the victim was lying and started the fire with a small disposable lighter.

Fortunately, because the fire was small and slow burning, the neighbors discovered it and called the police, who rescued the victim. When he recovered, he was able to recount what had happened to him.

Investigation and Capture

In most cases, the skeletal remains of victims damaged by fire remain intact, and any trauma occurring prior to the fire is visible and identifiable through an autopsy. An example of this is a gunshot wound to the head. When the skull is collected, it will show signs of the gunshot trauma, and a competent medical examiner can usually determine entrance and exit wounds along with distance determinations. (Distance determination measures the distance the weapon's barrel was from its target and eventual wound at the time of the shooting.)

When a sharp-force trauma, such as a knife wound, is inflicted, the bones of the victim yield the evidence of the trauma. We have seen skeletal remains that have not only suggested sharp-force trauma, but also revealed broken tips of knives embedded in the bone. This is easily identified at the time of autopsy through X rays of the remains.

When blunt-force trauma kills the victim, such as an assault with a baseball bat, the massive trauma that is left is clearly visible. When a person defends herself from someone striking her with an object, she suffers injuries such as broken bones to her fingers, hands, wrists and forearms.

TIP

Sometimes trauma wounds are misinterpreted by investigators. One little-known piece of information is that when a fire is of intense heat, the human skull's contents boil and explode much like a hard-boiling egg that is left unattended. To the untrained eye, this has often been determined to be a gunshot wound or a wound caused by blunt-force trauma.

Additionally, we have seen instances where, during the suppression of fire, firefighters caused trauma to the victims' bodies by walking into or kicking them. And when the firefighters are performing the overhaul, which is the cleanup after the fire, they sometimes damage the victims' bodies with axes, picks and shovels. This is done unknowingly, since the victims are either burnt beyond recognition or covered with fallen ceiling, walls and furniture.

F O U R

NARCOTICS MURDERS

Narcotics users come from a variety of backgrounds, from the street level junkie to the sophisticated smuggler. Statistics indicate that narcotics users are getting younger and younger.

In low-income areas, narcotics abuse is prevalent for a number of reasons. It is a business in which people with little education can make easy, fast money; it is a release for the user to escape his environment; and for the user who was reared in an environment of narcotics abuse, it is a way of life.

Middle- and upper-class users, frightened by the dangers of intravenous drug use in the age of AIDS, have started placing heroin into tobacco cigarettes, creating a new breed of Yuppie drug users.

While heroin use has increased, so also has the quality of the heroin. Early in Mauro's career when he was working as an undercover narcotics officer, heroin had a cut ratio of 3 to 7 percent heroin, with the rest being some sort of cutting agent, which can be any sort of white powder that looks like heroin; anything from talcum powder to rat poison is used. These cutting agents increase the volume of the heroin, thereby making it more profitable for the dealer. Today, narcotics officers inform us that street heroin—heroin bought by a user, not a dealer—is at least 75 percent pure. Because today's heroin is of such high quality, there is no longer a need to "cook" it.

TIP

Let's take a moment to discuss how heroin is typically used. It is usually purchased in small glassine or heat-sealed plastic bags, probably measuring an inch high and a half-inch wide. Each package is stamped with a name such as Viper, Homicide, Tombstone or Colt 45; or with some sort of design, such as a cross or a lightning bolt; or perhaps with some combination of name and design. This is the dealer's trademark, which tells the user what quality of heroin he is buying.

The user's "works" include a syringe, usually the type used in hospitals. The homemade needles common in the past are found only in prisons today, where inmate addicts may use an eyedropper with a needle made from a lightbulb filament. The user also has some type of tourniquet to help in exposing the veins. The tourniquet can be anything from a belt to a rubber band to a piece of string.

The user places the heroin in a spoon or bottle cap, where it is mixed with water so the powder liquifies. When the heroin is of poor quality (contains a lot of cutting agents), it gets cooked by heating the spoon with a match or cigarette lighter. After the heroin is liquified, the user rolls up a piece of cotton or a cigarette filter and places it in the heroin. The user then places the needle in the cotton or filter and extracts the heroin into the syringe.

Currently, the drug methamphetamine, which is referred to by street names of speed and crank, is growing in popularity with teens and young adults. The "peppy" feeling the drug produces can last up to twenty-four hours, which seems to give today's youth the excitement they are looking for: the ability to stay up all night and consume as much alcohol as they want.

Street Junkies

A heavy narcotics user who is living on the street, in a shelter or in some other low-income area has to deal not only with the daily necessities of life but also the never-ending craving for his drug of choice. The bottom line is that he needs the money to support his addiction. It is very hard for a person with such an addiction to maintain a nine-to-five job, so he has to find his money on the street. We have actually seen people with habits of over five hundred dollars a day.

Motives

The narcotic user's circumstances dictate why and how he kills. For example, both male and female prostitutes who sell themselves to support their addictions say they place themselves in situations where killing is the only way out. In some cases, their customers, or johns, attempt to steal from them, assault them and, in some cases, kill them. In this situation, junkies may kill in self-defense.

Junkies may also kill when they are denied drugs. They are, of course, addicts, and their drug of choice is the most important aspect of their lives. They do what is necessary to feed the habit. Their motives for murder are often one of the following:

- Someone tries to steal their stash of drugs.
- Someone tries to cut off their supply of drugs.
- Someone tries to steal the money with which they plan to buy their drugs.
- Someone refuses to sell them drugs, perhaps dealers to whom the junkies are in debt for previous deals.
- Someone sells them bad drugs.

In a moment of intense need, the junkie's addiction overrides any sense of morality or fear of getting caught. Getting and taking the drug is the one clear goal, and nothing will get in the way.

During the fight caused by one of the above motivators, the junkie uses whatever weapon is available, such as furniture or pieces of wood or brick to throw at or otherwise injure his victim. Or the murder may be a matter of a simple strangulation. But the killing is mainly because of the abuse of the narcotics and some form of argument over possession, whether it be of money or drugs.

Methods

In one scenario, a female hooker may have a prearranged location, perhaps behind a building, in an alley or at a seedy hotel, to which she will escort her client. At one point during the performance, the john may become rough, making it necessary for the prostitute to defend herself.

The weapon of choice is a knife or a box cutter, which is a single-edged razor blade placed in a holder for ease of handling and concealability. (The weapon of choice used to be a carpenter's knife, but it was bulky and difficult to conceal.) If a box cutter is used, the john most likely incurs slashes on the neck and facial area. If a knife is used, he probably suffers from a combination of slashes and stab wounds, possibly leading to his death. When a knife is used, chances are the prostitute is a transsexual or a male homosexual dressed as a female, especially if there are a number of stabs or slashes on the victim's body.

In another possible scenario, a prostitute may attempt to take money from a john's pant pockets while performing oral sex on him. If she doesn't get away from him before he discovers his money is missing, a deadly confrontation could occur.

Yet another possibility is when a street-level user attempts to perform a street robbery or burglary either by using a weapon or by threatening to use one. In this situation, victims are chosen according to the junkie's criteria, which usually includes the victim's vulnerability, the location, the time of day and the junkie's urgency to "score."

These street-level attacks typically occur on the first day of the month since most social service agencies mail recipients' checks on or near this date, thereby increasing the likelihood of low-income people having money. The victim may be approached in a hallway of her apartment building or, if she is on the street, may be forced into an alley as the perpetrator attempts to conceal his actions.

The victim usually refuses the attacker's demands, resulting in the perpetrator stabbing the victim in the chest until she dies. He searches her pockets and purse, which he may or may not remove, depending on the time and his comfort range.

Inner-City Drug Dealers

This type of dealer, usually male, sees drugs as a business. He probably doesn't use them. He lives in an inner city neighborhood, often the one he was born in. He therefore is from the predominant ethnic group of the area and is known by the people who live there.

Through drug money, he is able to buy expensive clothes and cars, and the people of the area, especially children and teenagers, respect him for his wealth and success. The money also buys the dealer power, so people inside and outside of the neighborhood fear him, too. He will kill to protect and expand his business enterprise.

His success and power also attract people to him. Children begin working for him, delivering the drugs, when they are as young as ten years old. He offers them a sense of belonging and a feeling of power. He also pays them more money than they could find anywhere else. They offer him cheap labor. Also, since they're minors, if they get caught, they will not go to jail. And since they are both loyal to and fearful of the dealer, they will not betray him.

Motives

In inner-city areas where narcotics are sold to maintain a lifestyle, the dealer must protect his turf. There is always a threat of someone attempting to move in on his territory. Most street-level dealers in inner-city areas obtain narcotics from bigger suppliers, and then peddle their wares on the street corner.

Another serious threat to a drug dealer is someone attempting to steal from him. Someone stealing from a dealer may simply want the dealer's goods without paying for them, or the thief may steal the drugs to make a profit from the resale. The street-level dealer must worry about being robbed because ultimately he has to pay his supplier for the merchandise. His supplier won't care if he was robbed, or if the police arrested him and confiscated the narcotics as evidence; the supplier just wants his money.

Methods

When a drug dealer is killed by another dealer for control of the turf, it is a planned execution, and the killer usually has some type of backup. The victim is watched for vulnerability, and the killing may or may not be done covertly. If the killer wants to create a sense of power, he just walks up to the victim on the street and shoots him, perhaps when his back is turned. Another possible method of murder is a drive-by shooting, which is described in the chapter on gang murder. Since the main motivation here is to eliminate the competition, the victim will not be robbed.

In the case of a theft that is orchestrated by the drug user when he is desperate for drugs and cannot come up with the necessary funds, he uses his familiarity with the drug dealer to build a false sense of security. He takes the dealer to a remote location, such as an alleyway. Since the dealer will want to find someplace private to make the deal, this should not be difficult. Then, when our drug dealer least expects it, the user stabs him in the chest numerous times until he is dead. If the user is following the dealer into a building or alleyway, he may stab him repeatedly in the back until the victim dies.

Keep in mind that the junkie is looking for drugs the dealer currently has in his possession. So when the victim is found, his pockets will have been searched and his cash and narcotics removed.

Casual Drug Users

Casual drug users tend to be middle-class older teenagers to young adults. Though heroin use is becoming more popular among this segment of the population, "recreational drugs" are used most often. Murders involving this type of user tend to occur at parties where the guests are under the influence of a narcotic, frequently methamphetamine. This drug, as mentioned earlier, is popular among the teen and young adult crowd because it keeps the user awake and active for twenty-four hours.

The user can literally "party all night long."

Unfortunately, the drug also causes irritability and impaired judgment and very often violent behavior. The sleep-deprived, nerve-frayed user is quick to argue and fight, and sometimes, to kill.

Motives

Motives for murder involving this type of drug user vary with the drug of choice. As mentioned above, methamphetamine creates an irritable and violent user. This user can start a fight over anything and end the fight by killing. The murder may stem from something as simple as an argument in which someone is insulted to a more serious situation, such as a rip-off or a suspicion of being a police informant.

These latter motives occur more frequently when the user prefers heroin. Other common heroin-user motives for murder:

- cover up a theft done to get money to buy the drug
- stop an informant from going to the police
- stop someone from informing a teenager's parents about the drug use

Since these drug users are from middle-class and upper-class families, the motive for murder is usually not profit oriented.

Methods

A typical scene is a group of speed addicts, or "crankheads," sitting around in the backyard of one of their residences, when a comment is made (perhaps a reference to one's girlfriend) and a fight ensues. This fight is basically hand-to-hand and continues until one is overpowered or the fight is broken up.

If the user (i.e., the drug addict) is attacked at his own residence, he goes inside the house to obtain a weapon (often a shotgun used for hunting) and returns to the yard to shoot his assailant. If the loser of the fight is not at his residence, he drives home to get a weapon and return to the scene for revenge.

The weapon is usually shot more than once, and others may or may not be killed at that location; much will depend on how they react to the situation. For example, someone who attempts to stop the gunman either by force or by calling the police may find himself in danger of being murdered as well, depending on the level of the perpetrator's rage.

If the killing is done for a more serious reason, such as avenging a drug theft or covering up the perpetrator's involvement in this activity, a lot more planning occurs because the victim has to be placed in a comfortable surrounding where he would have had no problem either arriving or being taken. For example, the victim, a suspected informant, may be told he is riding along to pick up drugs or is going to a party in some remote area. If the victim is trying to find information to report to the police, he goes along.

Let's say the word is out that Peter was recently arrested for possession with intent to sell narcotics. It is also known that Peter was released from jail without difficulty. So our drug dealers are suspecting Peter of being an informant for the police.

If Peter is an informant, he may have volunteered to assist the police in their drug investigation in exchange for leniency at time of sentencing. As volunteer informant, Peter could provide a variety of services, such as notifying law enforcement officers of location, time and persons involved with a drug arrival, making introductions to known drug dealers, or just providing basic intelligence of who is selling what type of drug, who is buying and using, where stashes are located and so on.

Because drug dealers fear their own arrests, they feel they must kill the suspected police informant. We have seen this done many ways, at many locations and with many different weapons. In one scenario, the informant is taken to a prearranged location, perhaps another dealer's place of business or residence. The victim is secured to a chair by ropes, chains or handcuffs and beaten until he tells how much information was revealed. At the conclusion of the interrogation, he is shot a few times in the head at close range. If he had been taken to a remote location, he will probably be left there. We have seen cases where informants were taken on board boats, where they were shot and thrown overboard.

Lower-Class Addicts

This type of addict is usually Caucasian and from a broken family. Often the single parent works at a low-paying job. The user, who could be male or female, started out at a young age abusing alcohol and marijuana and gradually drifted to harder drugs. Their friends are from similar backgrounds.

These addicts support their habits by selling drugs for more powerful dealers or by shoplifting or committing burglaries. They have no ambitions to become rich selling the drugs and probably will be lifelong users. They usually have only a few days' supply of drugs and are therefore always on the hunt for more. They are usually in poor health and give little thought to personal appearance. These are people with little hope or ambition of any kind in life and no morals. They are compulsive liars and scam artists. We have seen this type of user steal from a baby sister's piggy bank and cash a widowed mother's social security check.

Motives

When the drug-addicted person kills to obtain financial resources to purchase narcotics, this is usually done for two reasons. The most common one occurs during a robbery. The user loses control of the situation—perhaps the victim surprises the addict during the act or refuses to turn over the money during a robbery—and the user commits the murder to regain control.

The second most common motive is that the influence of the narcotics or the addiction is so overwhelming the user intentionally looks for someone to kill for a quick buck.

Methods

Let's look at the first scenario, in which a victim of robbery resists and the user resorts to violence to achieve her objective. Keep in mind that narcotics users are the most street-smart of all criminals. Their lives are based on getting drugs and getting high. So their modus operandi is to target the weakest victims and rob them when they have the most money.

In one situation, the user follows a female or elderly person to a location, such as a store, where she may be preparing to spend some money. Another strategy, which seems to be gaining popularity among narcotics users, is to wait across the street from an Automatic Teller Machine (ATM) while a person is accessing her account. The addict waits until the person is inside, if it's an enclosed ATM, or until she exits. There are times when the user inserts something such as a stick between the door and its frame or applies a piece of duct tape over the lock to ensure the door does not close or lock properly.

Once the money is withdrawn, the perpetrator overtakes the victim, either by physical force or with a weapon (such as a knife or a handgun), robs the victim and demands the ATM card and the PIN. Then the addict beats, stabs or shoots the victim and removes all forms of identification so the police cannot identify her. The perpetrator uses the ATM card over and over again.

TIP

The police can easily arrest such a perpetrator since all ATM locations contain at least one video recording system that records the person's face when she is removing money.

Midlevel Narcotics Dealers

This dealer usually supplies the street drug dealers with their narcotics. All races and backgrounds are found at this level. Most often, this dealer is male and views drug use as a business. He is not a user; he is a distributor. He buys narcotics in large quantities and uses cutting agents to increase the volume of the drugs before selling them to the street dealers.

This type is more powerful and more remote than the street dealer and is therefore more difficult for the police to apprehend. He is savvy and ruthless. He usually owns some type of legitimate business, such as a neighborhood bar or auto body shop, and he uses this setup to launder the drug money. This business also provides space to store the large shipments of drugs.

Motives

There is a lot of easy money to be made in narcotics dealing, and this money seems to corrupt some individuals in such a way that they are willing to kill for it. Eliminating people believed to be informants, punishing someone over missed payments or failure to deliver supplies, attempting to achieve a greater position in an organization (or to overthrow the organization), and even removing law enforcement personnel who are "getting too close" or creating obstacles are all motives for the narcotics dealer to murder.

Methods

Because midlevel narcotics dealers are capable of paying for the services of hit men, it is not uncommon for others to do the killing for the dealers. So the connections between the perpetrators and the victims, and the locations and methods of killing will vary. One thing is certain: The methods of killing will be more cruel and sophisticated than those used by lower-level dealers. Like other organized crime groups, they maintain or have access to personnel whose main function is enforcement. Intimidation and discipline are the key components in the governments of these organized narcotic rings. Killing is just one method for maintaining the status quo.

The weapons they utilize will be state-of-the-art automatic pistols, submachine guns and, in some cases, military assault weapons (see chapter two, Weapons of Murder).

The following example illustrates how organized drug gangs will enforce discipline to the point of murder. Drug smugglers have a lot to lose if they are apprehended by law enforcement. When they are caught with large quantities of narcotics, they face extremely long sentences, including life in prison.

Through the RICO (Racketeer Influenced and Corrupt Organization Act) statutes, all illegal profits and all items purchased with those profits can be retained by law enforcement and auctioned off, and all monies recovered from these auctions will be utilized to finance the war on drugs. The dealer, needless to say, is anxious not to get caught.

Scenario: Organized Drug Gang

Let's say Joey P. becomes a member of a drug gang. He starts out small by going to drop zones (places where drugs or merchandise is left as part of the delivery). These deliveries are secretive operations usually conducted in remote locations, such as a wooded area or a coastline, where drug gangs can carry out their activities undetected.

Suppose Joey P. is advised of this prearranged location. His function is to unload bails of marijuana from the transport plane to awaiting vehicles, which, once loaded, are driven to a central storage area for distribution of the drugs.

TIP

If a drug smuggler uses a single-engine airplane to transport a drug shipment, he removes all unnecessary equipment, including the seats, except the one used by the pilot. The narcotics, whether marijuana or cocaine, are placed completely around the pilot in such a way that he will be unable to exit his plane without some of the narcotics being removed by the ground personnel. This is done so the smugglers can transport as much product as possible at one time. In addition, since extra fuel tanks are installed to make this a long, nonstop flight, it is necessary to get rid of any nonessential equipment.

Up to this point, Joey P. has done everything that has been asked of him and done it in a professional manner. He is slowly making his way up the ranks as a trusted employee and is placed in charge of distribution and collection of some of the product. He's doing a fine job until all that quick money in his pockets begins to corrupt him. Joey P. buys a flashy, new, expensive sports car, he purchases a new house right on the ocean, he likes expensive and flashy jewelry and he is always seen with a beautiful young woman on his arm.

The police are made aware of Joey P. and start an investigation to determine how this chimney sweeper has managed to attain such a lavish lifestyle in a short period of time. Joey P. is even starting to abuse some of his own product, and his co-workers are becoming concerned about all the attention Joey P. is attracting. So they decide to take care of the situation.

Joey P.'s punishment will be swift and meaningful. It is intended not only to silence the problem but also to send a warning to others who may think of acting in the same manner. A number of scenarios could take place, but here we will list the most common ones we've seen.

The first would be to make an early morning arrival at

Joey P.'s house, around 3 A.M., when they know he will be fast asleep. How they arrive will depend upon several circumstances, including the location of his residence, the number of people present there, the security installed at the house and the approximate location of neighbors.

Because of the elaborate alarm system installed in Joey P.'s residence, the members of the drug gang decide to acquire the services of a coke whore. A coke whore is a person who will do anything for free narcotics; in this case, sex for cocaine. Her mission is to open the rear door once Joey P. is fast asleep to let in the assault team.

The team may consist of one to five members of the drug gang, remembering that they are trying not to draw any more attention than necessary to the situation. Once they are inside, Joey P. is awakened, given a few last words, perhaps assaulted a little and then shot. These gunshot wounds will be precise, probably to the head with a semiautomatic handgun. And if needed, a silencer may be used.

The female assistant is also shot and killed in the same manner. The assassins probably wear dark street clothes and gloves but leave their faces exposed. This may be done for two reasons: The first is so the victim sees and knows why he is going to die, and the second reason is to draw little or no attention to the assassin. Once their job is finished, the assassins leave the same way they entered.

In some cases, they may attempt to conceal the main purpose of the killing by making Joey P.'s residence look as if it were burglarized. This is achieved by prying open a rear door or a window to show a different point of entry than the original unlocked door. The victims' bodies will remain in the same locations in which they were killed.

In another possible scenario, Joey P. lives in a high-rise apartment with his family, which includes children. In this case, because of the potential for being discovered, our assassins enter the apartment midmorning or late afternoon. During these hours, most people are at work and their children at school, and other possible witnesses are involved with daily chores.

A person with whom Joey P. will be comfortable knocks on the door, and once the door is opened, the other assassins force their way in. Any family members in the apartment are gathered into a room and systematically murdered execution style—in the front, back or side of the head. Young children present, who, because of their ages, will be unable to identify the assassins, are spared.

We often also discover the victim dumped at a remote location where he may or may not have been killed. Before his murder, the victim may have been asked to perform a duty, such as to assist in transportation of the product. Once the assault team arrives at the remote location, the victim is shot at close range, killed and left in the position in which he falls.

There have been cases where victims were found bound and gagged and showing other signs of torture. This kind of evidence, however, usually indicates a drug rip-off or a robbery rather than a drug gang killing a member. In an actual case, victims were found by a teenage daughter when she returned home from school. Her father was a drug dealer who had ripped off his supplier by taking a shipment without paying for it. The girl's family members were bound and gagged with rope and duct tape, and the house was completely ransacked.

TIP

Ransacking is used for two different situations: (1) in an actual robbery and (2) when a killer creates a scene to look like a robbery occurred. Lately, we have been noticing that ransacking is performed in two methods. The first is characterized by complete and total chaos in which all drawers are emptied on the floor, furniture is moved and thrown about and every nook and cranny has been searched for loot. When we see this type of behavior, we tend to believe it is a juvenile or an inexperienced criminal. This type of search is very time-consuming and noisy, so detection is more likely. With the other method, the professional criminal only searches areas where the coveted item is most likely to be located. Take a second and think about where all your valuables are located. They are not placed all around the house. You do not put your best diamonds in the medicine cabinet. Professionals know this. They are looking to get in and out undetected.

Investigation and Capture

The first thing the forensic team tries to establish is a feasible point of entry or exit. The unlocked opened door will surely point out that an accomplice has unlocked it or that Joey P. knew his killers and let them in. To reconstruct the crime scene, the forensic team will first do a strategic cursory walk-through of the crime scene. This initial search is the recognition phase of crime scene investigation. The purpose is to recognize evidence. The reconstruction of the crime scene is one of the last functions performed and may not be completed, in some cases, until the autopsy is performed and reports of lab analysis are completed.

F I V E

GANG MURDERS

Street gangs in the United States began forming in the early 1920s in major cities on the East Coast. They started as ethnic gangs that congregated in large urban areas. As the population of poor and oppressed people grew nationwide, so did the number of street gangs. In the 1980s, gang membership increased dramatically, to the concern of law enforcement officials.

In 1996, 73 percent of the police workload in large urban areas, such as New York City and Chicago, was gang-related crimes; 45 to 55 percent of police work in smaller communities is related to gang crimes. Firearms are involved in 83 percent of the current workload, and a good portion of this is due to firearm availability to gangs and juveniles. In comparing the rate of violent crimes against the person (e.g., assault) and/or property (e.g., burglary), statistics show that juvenile crime continues to rise while all other violent crimes seem to be declining or holding at a steady level.

Neighborhood street gangs are typically broken down into three parts: gang members (sometimes referred to as gangbangers), the gang affiliation and the nongang members. Other terms for street gangs are posses, gangsters, crews and homeboys.

Gang Violence

In the beginning, gang members assaulted and killed one another for control of what they considered their property, or turf. Turf is usually a section of a city where a gang is located.

Rival gang members then began to seek revenge through the disrespect or damage of one another's property or members. One way gangs mark their turfs is by "tagging" buildings, dumpsters, mailboxes and so forth within their turfs. These tags look like meaningless graffiti, but to other gangs, they are "no trespassing" signs or street "newspapers" that keep members informed. One way rival gangs show disrespect for each other is by writing over, or x-ing out, another gang's tags or entering its turf. And each gang has its own set of colors or type of clothing that show membership, so rival gangs can show their disrespect by wearing the other gang's colors and clothing. This is why you sometimes hear of innocent youths getting killed because of the clothes they were wearing; the killers were members of a gang that wore the same type of clothes as a uniform, and they believed the nongang member was showing them disrespect.

Much of today's gang violence seems to occur because of the large profit to be made from drug distribution. The rival factions are fighting for control of another gang's drug profits. And since drugs bring in large amounts of money, gangs are able to afford bigger guns and more of them.

Organization

On the surface, all street gangs are formed to give the members a sense of belonging. As they expand, both financially and through membership, their ideology shifts from a sense of brotherhood to a focus on obtaining power, control and money. Once the gang achieves financial success, it grows and spreads throughout the United States to form a major organization, much like an organized crime group. The Crips and the Bloods, rival gangs once limited to the Los Angeles area, have now grown so large they have branches in almost every major city in the United States.

Most gangs are structured like a large corporation, with chains of command and members serving highly defined roles. They may even encourage violence among smaller street gangs to draw the attention away from themselves, thereby remaining invisible to law enforcement. It is not uncommon for extremely large street gangs to absorb smaller gangs with similar ideologies.

Since gangs have a significant presence in Los Angeles, many people think street gangs are a problem only in that city. The fact is, however, that organized street gangs can be found in just about every major urban area in the United States, and they are rapidly infiltrating small Midwestern towns.

And although drugs are a big part of gang life, street gang crime is not always narcotics related. Street gangs commit a wide range of crimes:

- carjacking and automobile theft
- possession of illegal firearms
- armed robbery
- burglary
- loan sharking and money laundering
- extortion
- kidnapping
- homicide

Current gang activity can be compared to that of the more organized crime groups established in the 1920s, such as the Italian and Irish mobs in and around New York City.

Juvenile Crime Groups

The current rise in juvenile crime can be attributed in large part to the rise of street gangs. In 1985, as the children of the baby boomers became adolescents, juvenile crime skyrocketed. Statistics show that since that time, the number of juveniles committing homicide has doubled. The number of homicides committed by juveniles with firearms has also doubled, as has the number of juvenile drug offenses.

Some professionals relate this increase in juvenile drug crimes to the increase of drug trafficking by children. We feel this is directly related to the ever-increasing number of children joining street gangs. Children are easily recruited to sell narcotics because they will work for much less than an adult and, if arrested, are less likely to do any significant jail time.

Children or cliques of children who kill may not necessarily constitute a street gang, but because they behave similarly, they are often classified as such. When a group of children is consistently hanging out in one location, the law enforcement community must decide whether the group is a street gang or just a group of neighborhood friends. The police utilize four criteria in making this decision:

1. the name or names of a leader or leaders

2. a known area or location where this gang continues to appear

3. the street gang's movement into crime such as narcotics selling

4. the association of itself in committing these crimes (e.g., gang members placing an "X" through the name—written in graffiti—of a rival gang member, indicating they have killed him)

When a group of teenagers associate closely for a prolonged period of time, differences in opinion may arise, which often result in violence. An example of this is the Hail Mary Boys, so named by the press because they were praying just prior to the crime. This group of friends decided to kill one of their buddies because they were unhappy with his childish behavior. While seated in a vehicle with the victim up front, the group began praying. While the victim had his head bent and eyes closed, an extension cord was looped around his neck, whereby he was strangled. The Hail Mary Boys evinced no gang behavior; they just decided to kill their childish friend.

Similarly, another group of boys targeted one of its

members for an execution-style murder. In this scenario, they took him to a secluded wooded area, not far from his home, where he was beaten to death with stones and a baseball bat. This kind of murder happens more and more, and the motivations are not gang related. Perhaps the victim publicly embarrassed one of the group's members or the whole group, or stole someone's girlfriend. Or it could be an occult influence. Although the motive may have been similar to the motives of a street gang, the killers were not members of a gang.

These types of murders even occur among girls. There have been documented cases of teenage girls killing each other over boyfriends or for status. In one such case, three girls brought their victim to an abandoned building where they first attempted to beat her with their hands and then switched to sticks and pipes found in the abandoned house. At one point, all three girls pulled out knives (taken from their homes) and stabbed the victim forty-three times.

Recruitment

Most lower-middle-class and middle-class children who join street gangs do so because of peer pressure and the perceived excitement of being in a gang; others seek to satisfy a need for security that may be missing at home. It is no coincidence that most hard-core street gang members come from dysfunctional families. For urban youth, a street gang can supply a place to live, a structured lifestyle, food, clothing and a sense of belonging. When working for a street gang, one can feel a sense of accomplishment for a job well done.

Some law enforcement and human resources professionals blame the upsurge in gang violence on the media's glorification of violence, sex, wealth and power. They discuss low-income inner-city children as having low self-esteem and no escape from the despair of poverty. The perceived power a gangster feels when he is in control of a violent situation adds to the notoriety of street gangs. This is why firearms play a key role in street gang lifestyle.

Recruiters in street gangs look for adolescents with minimal social and academic skills, knowing these will be the easiest to attract to membership. Most street gang members are high school dropouts. Statistics show that around 15 to 20 percent of street gang recruitment is achieved through intimidation factors and the rest is through friendships, families and, of course, the lure of money from dealing drugs.

Some gangsters are even born into membership. Street gang membership can be a family affair with brothers, sisters, aunts, uncles and cousins all belonging to the same gang. There is little or no recruitment necessary to find new members in these types of gangs because the social makeup of the family and the street gang intertwine, creating the only life one knows.

Ethnicity

Ethnicity often plays a role in gang formation, since much of the inner-city population is composed of recent immigrants. Low incomes, lack of a father figure in the household and a distrust of anyone not in their ethnic group causes these people to band together. Two of the most common are the African-American and the Latino groups, but there is growing concern about the new breed of street gangs that is organizing largely because of the money they can make from drug trafficking. Some of these new ethnic gangs are Vietnamese, Asian, Nigerian, Pakistani, Colombian and Iranian. We'll take a detailed look at Asian gangs later.

Because of the threat of rival ethnic street gangs, these young gang members pack handguns for protection when carrying considerable amounts of narcotics or money. Firearms are also considered status symbols, in much the same way certain brands of sneakers or other articles of clothing are status symbols for youth.

Initiation

Some street gangs have membership requirements for would-be members. These requirements are for both male and female initiates, with no exceptions. In one type of initiation, a female is forced to have some sort of sexual encounter with every gang member who requests it. In another type, an initiate is physically assaulted by a group of gang members.

It is worth noting that even child gangsters are fearless and seem to be willing to do anything—including commit murder—to belong to a gang. They devote their lives to the gang and the activities surrounding it.

Asian Gangs

Asian street gangs are generally based in the Chinatown sections of large cities. Whether they be Vietnamese, Chinese, Cambodians or others, they are typically spin-offs or branches of larger organized Asian gang families.

These types of street gangs typically serve the more established Asian gangs families (see chapter six, Organized Crime Murders) as drug couriers, number runners, enforcers and extortion collectors. Asian gang members often just walk up to a noncomplying victim and shoot her and everyone else who may be unfortunate enough to be a witness.

One scenario may be a Chinese take-out eatery whose owner has not paid her monthly protection money. The gang member walks in, demands the money and, even after it is turned over, shoots the owner in the head with a handgun. As is true with other gangbangers, the semiautomatic, high-capacity magazine is a favorite with the Asian gang member. After the deed is done, he just turns and walks out.

Within the Asian gang network, each culture maintains its own identity. For example, Japanese gangs' traits and customs are different from those of Korean or Vietnamese gangs. Chapter six, Organized Crime, explains how the Asian gangs' older, more organized brothers operate.

One of the oldest known Vietnamese organized street gangs calls itself the Frogmen, since during the war the members trained as underwater demolition experts, similar to our Navy Seals. They brought this training to U.S. shores to enhance their criminal activity.

Vietnamese street gang members range in age from early teens to mid-twenties. The gangs themselves are loosely organized and may or may not associate with other Asian street gangs. But they have no fear in stepping on or violating another Asian gang's turf for their own monetary gains. They tend to be mobile and are also very violent, using automatic weapons to perform their deadly deeds. They travel from city to city working out of or even taking over other Asian street gangs' safe houses, or locations where gang members can go to hide from the law. For example, they will move in on a Korean massage parlor (a front for a Korean prostitution ring), extorting money and staying until they feel a need to leave. Most Asian street gangs exist by extorting money from legitimate or nonlegitimate businesses and the families connected to them.

Home invasion is becoming an increasingly violent method of extortion. In this method, the gang locates a home, steals a vehicle to use to drive to and from the victims' residence, and violently kicks open doors and windows in both the front and the rear of the house. Once entry is gained, a demand is made, and, in all likelihood, one or more of the victims is violently beaten or shot to death.

TIP

When writing about your Asian victims, it is important to remember their fear of the police and government. In our country, offenders have a right to bail. In a communist state, the only way to get out of jail is to bribe or cooperate with the officials. So being released on bail in the United States makes it look like the gang has the cooperation of the police, so the gang members go back to the victims and tell them that the reason the gangsters are out is because they have the police under control, just like in their homeland.

Another contributor to their fear is the fact that the Asians don't trust police officers who look and act differently than the Asians do. As mentioned before, some ethnic groups have a difficult time trusting anyone of a different ethnicity.

Note, too, that Asians have a strong belief in fate. It is not that they are not distressed over the loss of a loved one, but they determine it to be the workings of fate and they go on with their lives.

Motives

Gang members kill for a number of reasons, including for the thrill of it. This type of violence is common behavior for street gangs. In performing this grisly task, they feel a sense of belonging, as they show the other gang members they have what it takes to be one of them.

The gang murder motive we'll focus on here is revenge for an act of disrespect to a gang's street graffiti. For the experienced gang banger, graffiti is the street's newspaper. It tells about recent deaths, promotions of its members, people associated with the gangs and upcoming killings. Graffiti also includes a record of the killing of police officers who have caused problems for the gang.

When a gangster puts down his tag, which can be a symbol, his initials or a nickname, he is marking his turf. If a rival gang member places an "X" through the tag or writes something over it, he is showing a sign of great disrespect or threatening his rival. The punishment for such an act could be as severe as killing the perpetrator(s), and the gang members who were disrespected will lose no time in plotting a retaliation.

Every detail is carefully planned: which car will be driven (and whether it will be stolen, or one already in their possession); who the driver will be; who will carry out the shooting; where the shooting will take place; what weapons will be used; where the target will most likely be found; and where he will be killed. The location of the murder is a key element, since the gang wants to choose a spot that will have the most impact on their rivals. Once these details are arranged, the plan is set in motion.

Methods

Gang members typically avenge the disrespect of their turf by committing a drive-by shooting at the rival gang's weekly celebration. Their intelligence reports that there will be a social gathering at a rival member's residence. One might wonder how, if these street gangs are so tightly bonded, this party information leaks out. Police officers who patrol gang areas inform us that most of the information is obtained through the gang members' girlfriends (if male gangs) and associates.

Now back to the party. The plan is to wait until the party is in full swing so the partygoers are somewhat intoxicated and their defenses are down, making it easier to perform the drive-by without resistance. The driver positions his vehicle so the shooters on the passenger side, both front and back, are nearest to the residence of the rival. The gang may or may not send a scouting vehicle for reconnaissance purposes. This reconnaissance team's mission is to obtain information such as the strength or the number of members outside or any possible defense positioning or to simply verify the party is going on.

The reconnaissance vehicle usually contains the gangbangers' girlfriends, so as to not attract the attention of any of the partygoers. The party house will have its own surveillance underway, which may include lookouts on each corner or just in front of the house. Their job will be to alert the other members if they see anything suspicious.

Once the reconnaissance vehicle sees that a party is, in fact, going on, the action begins. The vehicle with the shooter slowly creeps toward its apparent target, and just prior to reaching the location, the shooters position their weapons out the windows and fire. It is not uncommon to have the person sitting behind the driver crouch in the open window and fire over the roof of the vehicle. The shooting continues until the magazines are emptied or the vehicle has removed itself from the intended target.

Another method is to send one car in to shoot up the location and then while the rivals are out assessing the damages, send a second vehicle past to spray an additional barrage of bullets upon them.

Not all such killings are drive-by shootings, however. Sometimes a murder is accomplished at school or in the mall by simply walking up to a rival gang member who has violated territorial agreements, pulling out a small-caliber handgun and putting it to the face of the victim.

Prior to the shooting, the assailant verbally abuses his victim by reminding him that he had violated turf policy, and there may even be a limited amount of pushing or punching. While all this is happening, fellow gang members egg him on. The shooting itself is quick, with two or three shots to the face and body. Upon the completion of the gang member's duty, he flees the area with his brother gangbangers, either on foot or by vehicle.

Weapons

In drive-by killings, the weapons of choice are fast firing and able to hold large numbers of rounds. Concealability is not a concern. Twelve-gauge shotguns, both semiautomatic and pump action, could be used. The barrels and stocks could be removed or shortened with a hacksaw. This is done for two reasons: to allow ease of movement in getting it from inside the vehicle to outside the window and to cause the pellets to spread, making a wider impact area. Most shotguns hold only six rounds of shells, so an extension tube may be added in an attempt to gain a higher magazine capacity.

The handguns commonly used in gang warfare are the .380, 9mm, .45 and even the new police cartridge, the .40 SW caliber round. All of these handguns are semiautomatic with a magazine capacity of at least ten rounds.

Small-caliber semiautomatic versions of submachine guns are also used. Machine pistols, such as Mac-10 or -11 or Tec-9, have barrels as short as three to six inches in length but are capable of carrying large-capacity magazines with at least fifty rounds per magazine.

A final choice is the semiautomatic version of the assault weapon, such as the AR-15, AK-47, SKS or the mini-14. These weapons usually fire a steel-jacketed bullet that will easily penetrate vehicles and walls of houses.

Street Gangs and Law Enforcement

It is a whole different story when it comes to these street gangs killing law enforcement personnel. Street gangs, unlike other criminal types, are fearless for a number of reasons. Some experts who investigate this phenomenon believe this is a product of their environment. These kids are reared in a lifestyle in which they are convinced, and rightfully so, that they will not live long enough to grow old. And because of this, they will perform their criminal behavior with reckless abandon.

Mauro once worked with a fellow who is now in a large metropolitan police force in Washington State and is presently in charge of the street gang unit there. In his jurisdiction, there is a large street gang dilemma. One of his responsibilities is to attend a function where the police and gang members work out their differences in a nonthreatening way. One time, he brought along his older son to assist gang members in working new computers that had been donated to the community center. He introduced the leader of one of the rival gangs to his son.

This tough gangbanger, who would kill you in an instant, kneeled down to the officer's son and said, "Your father and me come from different sides and I would never ask your father for anything. But I'll tell you one thing, listen to your father and do what he tells you to do because if you don't, you'll end up like me. And I can guarantee you that by the end of this month, somebody will probably kill me, and I know this and this is why I'm telling you this." Well, it took a little bit longer than he predicted, but around six weeks after this conversation, the violent gangbanger was shot by a rival gang as he was leaving his car to walk into his house. So when you are dealing with your characters, make sure you portray this true sense of hopelessness these gang members carry.

Because of this lack of hope, gang killers are reckless. Unlike many criminals, they will kill police officers. One case we remember occurred in a city with a large street gang population. This is worth noting since there is usually a great distrust of the police in areas with a history of street gangs.

A police detective in a street gang unit was making arrests on drive-bys and in drug deals and was even cracking down on gang graffiti. The officer, fully aware of the potential for violence, took an hour and a half every day to drive home, doubling back, getting off at different exits, pulling over and waiting, just to make sure no one was following him.

Because of his caution, the gangbangers couldn't maintain

TIP

One way to determine if someone is following you while you are driving your vehicle is to make four consecutive right turns and look in your rearview mirror to see if anyone is following you. It is just about impossible that someone else is making the same four right turns as you are to get to her location and not yours.

proper surveillance on him and tried other means. An article about the officer's child appeared in a newspaper, so our ingenious gangsters waited outside the child's school until the detective arrived to pick up his children. As he walked to the gate leading to the doorway where his children were exiting, the gangbangers performed a typical drive-by. With the officer's back facing them, they opened up with AK-47s, killing him in front of his children.

Hate Groups

A newly emerging class of street gangs is the hate group. Hate groups can be characterized by their belief in separation, that is, the separation of different races, sexual orientations or religious beliefs, or a perception that they are better than a different group of individuals.

Religious difference has caused conflict since the beginning of time, and it seems that this kind of conflict is being perpetuated today by hate groups. White hate groups, such as the Posse Comitatus and the Aryan Nation, use strong religious beliefs to justify their hatred and violence. They believe they have a duty to maintain their organizations' beliefs in dealing with "the enemy."

Many of these groups have a paramilitary organization, which supports their violence. The paramilitary division is responsible for training and for enforcing the chain of command and the plan of action, much like in a military structure. Training includes propaganda against different racial groups, similar to Hitler's propaganda against the Jewish people. Military training in which military weapons and tactics are employed, is also assigned to each member. Hate groups generally choose a leader who is responsible for directing the daily functions and missions of the group.

Most hate groups are not well funded and are usually sustained by membership donations. Financial support is also bolstered by fund-raisers, such as newspaper, magazine and T-shirt sales, bake sales and car washes. Sometimes they mask these events as a fund-raiser for something else, and sometimes they are bold enough to declare for whom they are raising money.

Hate groups recruit young members with low incomes and low self-esteem who are looking for a sense of belonging. They use rock music that promotes their ideology to help preach their philosophy of hatred.

One of the most well-known hate groups, the Skinheads, was influenced by punk rock music and has developed into a vicious racial hate group based on Nazi ideologies and white supremacy.

Skinheads usually wear a uniform, which is another form of intimidation, much like the brown shirts were, marching through Berlin when Hitler came to power. A major component of this uniform is black combat-type boots with multicolor laces. Each color represents a specific group or belief. These boots are also used to literally stomp a victim into submission, which can eventually lead to the victim's death. Skinheads also wear swastikas, decorate their bodies with disturbing tattoos, wear suspenders (which they refer to as "braces") and have short to closely shaven hairstyles.

Skinhead homicides are often spur-of-the-moment violent outbreaks resulting from a confrontation. Let's say some Skinheads are returning home from a rabble-rousing meeting and are "pumped up." They observe a young man whom they presume to be homosexual. They begin shoving him and taunting him with vicious remarks to incite a confrontation. If the victim attempts to ignore or walk away from this behavior, an effort is made to secure his presence by pushing or holding him there. The victim is eventually punched and kicked until he is forced to the ground.

Weapons of choice are easily carried items, such as concealable knives, chains, baseball bats, brass knuckles, pipes and military-style handguns and rifles.

One method of killing victims occurs during a protest march or rally where they carry their signs of hatred, but with a difference: These signs are made out of a heavy thick piece of wood, which, when the Skinheads are confronted, are turned into clubs to beat their victims. Such attacks are usually one-sided, as the victims show up to protest the hate group, unprepared to defend themselves.

It is also common for hate groups to carry out an

execution-style murder of one of their "enemies." They might abduct a lone victim, transport him (possibly in a van) to a remote location, beat and torture him to death and then move the body to a more visible location where it is hung from a tree. This is done to create both confusion and fear and is a popular practice of the IRA (Irish Republican Army). Abducting a lone British soldier on his way home from the pub, the IRA will kill him and dump his body in a public place.

An oddity of hate groups is their strong belief that what they are doing is the only solution for the American people. And despite the heinous nature of their crimes, they look down on drug and alcohol abuse.

Investigation and Capture

Investigation of these various gangs is difficult because of the loyalty members have for one another. These groups all believe in a common goal. Witnesses are few because they are intimidated by the possibility of themselves or family members being retaliated against. Detectives who investigate crimes involving gang members tell us their best informants are the girlfriends of the gang members. This is probably because they have children and are looking for a way out of gang involvement. Most arrests are made after grueling investigations, or when the police happen to be on routine patrol and observe the crime.

ORGANIZED CRIME MURDERS

Many organized crime groups operate throughout the United States, including some with international ties. When we think of organized crime, perhaps the first thing that comes to mind is the traditional Mafia, a crime family of Italian descent. Others you may think of are the Asian, Colombian and Russian syndicates. Just about every ethnic group can claim an organized crime syndicate, however, and today more new groups are showing up in newspaper headlines. Street gangs who have "graduated" to organized crime also fall into this category.

In the Beginning: The Camorra and the Mafia

The camorra, one of the oldest criminal organizations, began in Spain, later branching out into Italy, where it developed a stronghold in Naples and eventually spread throughout the country. The camorra began by recruiting Italian prisoners and training them to be professional thieves and hit men. As the camorra grew and strengthened during the nineteenth century, society's wealthy young men became interested and joined. This is the first recorded appearance of the dons, who ruled with an iron fist, killing all those who violated their loyalties to the organization.

In the 1930s, the Italian government began cracking down on the leaders of the camorra, forcing them to leave the country and make their way to the United States. Upon arriving here, they set up their secret societies in New York and New Jersey.

Based in Sicily, the Mafia began as a society to protect the tiny island from raiding Arabs and French. It quickly formed into a criminal enterprise, and its influence began to spread throughout southern Italy. Eventually the Mafia got resistance from the government, and in the mid-1920s, the Mafia was forced to flee Italy, making its way to America's newfound freedoms.

When they arrived in America, the camorra began to fight with the Mafia for control of the Italian neighborhoods located in large cities throughout the United States. These organized crime groups began and maintained their criminal enterprises by extorting monies and merchandise from businesspeople.

One technique used by both the mafioso and camorristas was the *la mano nera*, otherwise known as the black hand. With this procedure, the groups demanded monies or property from an owner of an establishment via a letter. Some of these were death threats against the merchant or his family and threats to burn down his establishment. These letters were signed with an image of a hand stamped in black ink.

Another group placed dead canaries in their victims' mouths to let the rival gang members know who was responsible for the killing. The same terror tactic was also used to intimidate newly arrived Italian immigrants in the United States. These early criminal operations helped finance the beginnings of the Mafia in our country.

Firearms were hard to obtain and expensive at that time, so these killers used knives, clubs or ropes to stab, beat or strangle their victims, as well as many other types of brute force.

Since many police of the period were corrupt and the field of crime scene examination was limited, many of these crimes went unpunished. It is also notable that the victims were immigrants and not pillars of society, so their cases were not considered "high profile."

TIP

Italians were not the only immigrants; other European immigrants settled in the slums of New York City. Polish, English and Irish immigrants in the lower East Side formed street gangs that fought for territories to control gambling, extortion, robbery and prostitution. The 1920s was a bloody time in New York City because of the many killings done by rival gangsters.

During Prohibition, organized crime made millions. Bootleggers of the Roaring Twenties illegally made, imported and distributed liquor to satisfy the thirsty patrons of the speakeasies. To gain control of the business, gangs carried out assassinations to eliminate rival gangs.

In the 1930s, the national syndicate was formed. The syndicate tried to consolidate and unify all of the organized crime families. The negative publicity generated by the different factions in their struggle for power forced law enforcement authorities to crack down on them. The various gangs developed a chain of command and implemented rules and regulations that included the division of territories and the maintenance of an enforcement group known as Murder, Inc. This group carried out assassinations for the syndicate. For more information about Murder, Inc., see chapter seven.

The chain of command supervised the crime families, creating stability and structure in the organization. One such chain of command still operating today is called the Honor Society, which breaks down the responsibilities of a crime family. Starting at the bottom is the *giovane d'honore*, who is an associate of the family and cannot advance because of his non-Italian heritage. Next up the ladder is the *picciotto*, commonly referred to as the button man. This low-ranking individual gains the respect of the family by being its enforcer. The foot soldier, or the *sgarrista*, takes a secret oath upon initiation into the family, and his responsibility is to maintain its daily business. He is referred to on the street as a mademan. Then come the lieutenants, referred to as *capodecina*. The *capodecina* maintain discipline and direct the *sgarrista*. The people responsible for carrying out the financial responsibilities of the crime family are the *contabilo*. Then there is the underboss, or *capo bastone*, who is actually the vice-president or the second in command. There is also an advisor or counselor who assists in family business. He is known as the *consigliere*. And at the very top is the boss, also known as *capo crimini*.

Now let's look at how organized crime members kill and get killed.

Case Study: The Death of a Mafia Mademan

Mauro grew up in a small town populated by people of mostly Irish and Italian descent. Some of his childhood friends' fathers were button men and mademen associated with a crime family out of New York City. Mauro admits to this day that these kids' lives were pretty good until "the ultimate" happened.

One of Mauro's best friend's father was well liked and respected in the neighborhood. He was an immaculate dresser, always wearing custom-made clothes, fancy jewelry and imported shoes. He drove around in a late-model Cadillac or Lincoln. When the ice-cream truck came, he bought ice cream for the children on the entire block, and everyone was amazed at the amount of money he would pull out of his pocket.

Then, the unthinkable happened. One day the father went out and never returned. His wife, being a good Mafia wife, never contacted the police. About a week later, his seven-year-old twin sons found him sitting in his car just two blocks from home. The twins realized something was wrong and ran home to get their mother. Upon reaching her husband, she knew her worst fears had come true: He was dead. The autopsy revealed that a ¾-inch galvanized pipe had been inserted into his rectum and forced up into his chest cavity.

The investigation revealed that a large quantity of heroin had been seized by the police, and the crime family believed the victim was responsible for the loss of the shipment. As you can see, there is no honor among thieves.

Unfortunately, the old saying "like father, like son" proves true here: Mauro's buddy became a mademan and was arrested in Texas for smuggling heroin into the United States. He was sentenced to life in prison.

Mob Killings

Motives and Methods

We'll start by describing why and how a hit is carried out. Let's say Joe BagofDonuts, who is a *picciotto* for a Mafia crime family, is suspected of either stealing from the family or being an informant against the family. Because of his present status, the family feels he has become a risk and must be eliminated.

BagofDonuts is contacted by another member of the family on the pretense of arranging a meeting for later that evening. Since the *picciotto* doesn't know what is about to happen to him, he is not in any way suspicious and will make no attempt to flee or resist. He either drives himself to the prearranged location or is picked up at his residence.

The pretense of this meeting could be to move stolen property, to discuss upcoming assignments or to simply have a friendly get-together. While at the location, the victim may be forced into another vehicle and taken to a remote location or killed right on the spot—we've seen both occur. The victim is taken to a remote location for two reasons:

1. There is less chance of the killer being apprehended or observed.

2. There is no need to dispose of the body—it will be left where it falls.

The weapon of choice in these types of killings is a handgun. It could be anything from a .22 caliber to a .40 SW caliber. The short 2- or 4-inch barrel revolver and the .38 caliber are most often used. This is probably because these guns are easy to obtain and conceal. Another reason why revolvers are used is because no shell casings are ejected and left at the scene for identification by the police. A silencer is sometimes used to suppress the sound of the gunshot if the killing is in an area where shots might draw attention. After the shooting, the murder weapon is wiped clean of fingerprints and disposed of as the killers leave the scene.

TIP

Shell casings are not left at the scene of the crime when a revolver is used. The only time they remain is when they are ejected from a semiautomatic pistol or the revolver is opened and emptied of its spent shell casings for a possible reload.

We have seen cases where the victim was taken to a remote location on the pretense of committing a burglary of a storage area or an establishment. Upon arrival, the shooter and the victim exit the vehicle and the shooter allows the victim to walk in front of him. When the shooter feels the time is right, he directs two carefully placed shots at the victim's head, killing him immediately. The victim is left where he falls. The shooter then disposes of his weapon, knowing it is a lot easier to dispose of a weapon than to be caught with it and have it traced to a murder through ballistic examination.

Keep in mind that money is no object for large organized crime families, so the replacement of weapons is not a concern. One method of disposal is to throw the gun out of the car window and into a river while passing over a bridge. Most handguns disposed of in this manner are never recovered, largely because the exact location of disposal is hard to pinpoint. To make matters worse, tidal currents and the softness of the sea floor cause the weapon to sink rapidly into the mud. And if there is only one person in the vehicle as it is disposed of, then he is the only witness.

Upon examining the scene, the only evidence to be found by the police are the projectiles in the victim's body. And sometimes the murderer doesn't even leave the corpse.

Disposing of the Body

The killer may attempt to conceal the body by tying concrete blocks to its torso and heaving it into a river, lake or ocean. In order to keep a body submerged in water for a period of time, the counterweight must be at least 10 percent more than the total body weight since, during its natural decomposition, the body forms gases that aid in raising it to the surface. Another method of keeping the body submerged is to puncture the torso to help release the naturally developing gases. The time it takes for the body to resurface depends on the water temperature and tidal current action. Eventually, it is these tidal currents that bring the body to the surface, no matter how securely it is weighed down.

Another method of disposing of the victim is to remove the limbs and head from the torso and bury the parts in various locations. This makes it difficult to identify the victim if only a part or parts of the body are found.

Burial at some remote or undetectable location is another possibility. There's a popular rumor that Jimmy Hoffa, the teamster official who's been missing for quite awhile, is buried beneath Giant's Stadium in New Jersey.

Killing the Crime Bosses

Motives and Methods

One reason mob killers assassinate their bosses is to gain control of the organization. Since the bosses are savvy and experienced, having likely orchestrated killings themselves, unique tactics must be employed in eliminating them. Crime bosses do not voluntarily go for rides to secluded areas; some type of force or threat is necessary.

Since the capos are well protected by bodyguards, the hits are usually carried out when least expected. For instance, the capo may be shot while eating at his favorite restaurant or as he enters his vehicle for the ride home.

These hits, which occur very quickly, are performed in the following manner: The capo's whereabouts are identified and he is approached by one or two assassins who pull out semiautomatic handguns and open fire, not stopping until the victim is completely lifeless. Of course, his bodyguards are also shot if they show any resistance. There have been times when the bodyguards were aware of the hit, and, as it is was going down, they just walked away from the area. By showing any defensive behavior, they too would have been shot.

In a different situation, a boss may be enjoying himself at a social club when he is forced from the club at gunpoint, taken to a remote waterfront location and gunned down by a few shots to the head.

Yet another way mobsters kill each other is with explosives. Small pipe bombs, for instance, may be placed underneath the seat of the victim's vehicle and set to explode when the ignition key is turned. One mobster who knew his enemies would try to use this technique to rub him out would have a sgarrista start his vehicle before he drove it. The only problem was that the mobster's enemies were aware of his precaution, so they set the bomb to explode when the vehicle's transmission was shifted into drive.

When the victim's vehicle is placed at a location where it is either protected or secured from any tampering, a different method is used. The mob killer follows the victim in his vehicle until he parks it. The killer then parks his vehicle next to the victim's vehicle so the passenger-side door of this car is parked right next to the victim's driver-side door.

The passenger-side door contains an explosive device with a radio frequency (RF) controlled detonator. When the intended victim approaches his vehicle and attempts to unlock his door, the nearby assassins transmit the detonating device to explode, killing him.

At one time, mob members would only retaliate against each other leaving the family members alone. But, around the 1980s, this trend seemed to have disappeared in some factions of the Mafia. Members who fought for control would kill other family members.

The Westies

The Westies, an Irish street gang that Mauro came to know as a child, started in the Hell's Kitchen section of Manhattan. The Westies are ruthless and became the enforcers when they joined forces with an Italian crime family out of New York. They often kill their victims by beating them to death with a club or a hammer, but they also use knives, sawed-off shotguns and small-caliber stub-nosed revolvers.

The Westies often grab the victim off the street, forcing him into their vehicle at gunpoint. They then drive to a remote location, beat the victim and shoot him several times. They may shoot him in the head while he is lying on the ground, just to make sure he is dead.

Asian Organized Crime Families

Asian gangs have been in existence for centuries. One such organization, the Chinese Triad Society, was developed to over- throw the Manchu dynasty. From the Triad Society, a number of smaller groups formed, such as the White Lotus Society. These smaller societies became the centers of organized crime in China and in the many countries throughout the world. Be- cause of Communist takeover, the Chinese Triads moved from their locations inside China to Hong Kong, Taiwan and Singa- pore. The large populations of Chinese immigrants in Hawaii and California have made it easy for the Triads to blend in there as well.

The Triad Society is responsible for drug trafficking, the smuggling of people out of China (who may or may not be used as prostitutes or indentured servants) and, of course, gambling. Triad members are ruthless and use extortion, which includes murder, to achieve their objectives. They use their enforcers, referred to as hatchet men, to make sure the Triad's wishes are carried out.

Motives and Methods

Chinese gangs generally kill to make a point. For instance, these gangs will make an example of a prostitute who refuses to work and attempts to flee. Before being killed, the victim is tortured in front of others. This is to drive home the point that any lack of cooperation is not tolerated.

Sometimes the Triads use carjacking to achieve their goals. They follow a driver of an expensive luxury vehicle and, when the vehicle is stopped at a light, force their way in at gunpoint, keeping the victim inside. At some point during the carjacking, the victim is shot and dumped from the vehicle. The vehicle is then shipped to China where it is sold for many times the original value.

When the Triad is attempting to extort money from a businessperson, its members are equally ruthless. First, they demand their price, and if it is not received, they abduct a member of the businessperson's family. Then they have the victim talk to his family over the telephone and the demand is repeated. If the ransom is still not produced, the victim is tortured, killed and dumped on the doorstep of the business. This type of murder is common around the time of the Chinese New Year, when it is customary for the Chinese to keep large sums of cash in their homes for good luck and financial success throughout the coming year.

Another way the Triad obtains money is more blatant—and bloodier. The killers follow a prominent businessowner home and force him into his own house at gunpoint. They then round up the family members in one room and demand that all monies and jewelry be turned over to them. If this demand is not met, a family member is either shot or stabbed to death. They continue to demand the family's valuables and kill a family member each time they are denied. Even after the demands are met, there is still a strong possibility that all family members will be killed.

The Fuk Ching

Like other moneymaking organizations with spin-offs, organized crime groups have their own copycats. One example is a small but notorious Chinese gang of Fujianese people known as Fuk Ching. The Fuk Ching have a history of holding recent Asian-American immigrants for large ransom payoffs. The only catch here is that the payoffs must be made by the relatives in mainland China.

The Fuk Ching gang may remove fingers from the victims to be sent back to their relatives to prove they are holding the victims hostage. The longer the demand for money is not met, the more violent the gangsters become.

It is not unusual for the members of the Fuk Ching gang to torture the victim while they are asking for the ransom payments. The longer the gang members have to wait, the more violent the assaults become. One victim was bound, tortured and strangled, and after she was dead, a heavy television set was used to crush her skull. The gang mutilated a number of these Chinese immigrants, who were found deceased, to send a message to their nonpaying relatives. It is also common for this gang to kidnap more than one victim, kill one of them by a gunshot to the head and then dump the body on a major street or highway so the authorities can find it.

Paying the ransom, however, does not always guarantee the victim will be released safe and sound. There have been times when the kidnapped victim was shot and the apartment where the victim was located was set ablaze.

Japanese Organized Crime

One Japanese organized crime family is known as the Yakuza. This crime family initially overthrew the samurai warlords and dates back to around the 1600s. The gang members are easily identified because their entire bodies are tattooed with detailed drawings of serpents.

Yakuza members are extremely loyal to their bosses and have been known to sever their own fingers to show their support. In the chain of command of the Yakuza, the bosses have total control over the membership. These members control a large number of legitimate businesses in Japan today.

The Yakuza are known to carry handguns, despite strict gun control laws in Japan. They control prostitution, gambling, narcotics and the importing and exporting businesses. They have been known to branch out and join forces with the Chinese Triads, forming a formidable narcotics trafficking operation.

The Yakuza have been known to work with other crime families throughout the world but are based primarily in Japan.

Russian Organized Crime

With the fall of the Communist party in the former Soviet Union, Russian organized crime has begun to flourish and thrive. There are many explanations for this; some believe this organized crime is being sponsored and supported by former KGB members who still maintain a certain status and power in Russia today.

Russian organized crime deals with extortion of business owners for protection. The mobsters demand money from business owners, and if the money is not obtained, the business owners are shot and killed. It is easy for these criminals to obtain weapons. They use Russian military weaponry and can easily outgun the local police.

The Russian Organizatsiya, just as the other ethnic organized crime families, has made its way to America. The groups have set up shop in areas where other Russian immigrants live. The local immigrants are very fearful of them, but because of the distrust of the police that they bring with them from their homeland, they seldom seek assistance.

As in Russia, these crime families in the United States are well armed and well structured. They usually enforce their regulations by killing, which is done in a similar manner to the hits described earlier in this chapter. They forcibly apprehend their victim, bring her to an area where they feel secure and shoot her, leaving the body where it lies.

In cases where the victims are killed and have to be moved to another location, they are cut up with chain saws, axes and large butcher knives into small portable pieces, placed in plastic bags and transported to remote locations to be dumped. If there is a body of water nearby, they usually dispose of their victims' body parts there.

Other Organized Crime Groups

The members of other organized crime families, especially those established from small street gangs, are usually united by race or place of origin. These groups, of which the Colombian drug cartels are only one example, tend to be very violent in nature.

Motives and Methods

Members of these groups use violence for enforcement purposes and for gaining control over territories and contraband.

Their old ways of drive-by shootings are still used, but they also hire killers.

These hired or contracted killers may be associates of theirs or a local street gang. Prior to killing their victims, they violently assault them.

Most killings are used to conceal illegal activities the members may be involved in. Let's say that local residents complain about the large volume of people who enter and leave a house or building in their neighborhood. The police crack down and make an arrest. The group that was running the house may retaliate by burning down one of the complainant's homes. This is not done for revenge, but rather to warn the locals about going to the police again, once the group establishes another such meeting place. If the victim's family is killed in the fire, it makes for a more effective warning.

Investigation and Capture

When the police are investigating these organized crime murders, there may not be a lot of evidence located. Usually, these hit-and-run assaults leave few clues, and any eyewitnesses are so stunned or reluctant to testify that the murderers are seldom apprehended.

If the perpetrators of these murders are apprehended, it is usually because of electronic surveillance, recorded conversations or the testimony of a fellow member who wishes to avoid criminal prosecution himself.

The new breed of organized crime families has learned from the mistakes of its predecessors. The members are not as flamboyant, and they try to hide their illegal activities with legitimate ones. But they are more likely to kill anyone who stands in their way, and this type of killing is much more violent than that of their forerunners. Terror, intimidation and torture are their tools of control.

CONTRACT MURDERS

Of all the types of murderers in this book, the contract killer is the most emotionally and psychologically removed from the actual murder. A true contract murderer is a professional killer hired by a client to eliminate someone with whom the killer has no personal tie. In some cases, the killer may know the victim, but even so will not let personal feelings come between her and her assignment.

Unlike in crime-of-passion murders, serial murders, mass murders and sexual murders, the contract murderer has no psychological motivation for killing; her main motivation is greed. Contract killers kill for a price, although the price may be something other than money—perhaps guns, drugs, cars or simply the promise that something will occur after the murder takes place. An example of the latter may be a political assassination, after which the assassin's friends are released from prison or the assassin herself is given a position of power.

Profile

A contract murderer can be anyone: male or female, old or young, experienced killer or novice. The only real unifying factor is that these people are paid to kill. They are not hired to wound or scare people. They do not torture or stalk their victims. They are hired specifically to murder people, and they do so as quickly and easily as possible. Their goal is to get the job done and get paid.

There are many different types of contract murderers. Some, like Mafia hit men, kill strictly within their own organizations. Other contract murderers are available to anyone for the right price. Still others operate strictly on a recommendation basis and do not deal with strangers. Some use high-tech weaponry, while others simply beat a person to death.

Many contract murderers have military, law enforcement or covert operations backgrounds. They are quite familiar with weapons and have the ability to move into an area that is unknown to them, perform the assignment, then get out quickly and undetected.

Professional contract murderers are able to blend into unfamiliar surroundings easily; if they stand out, the chance is greater that someone will notice them and be able to describe them to police later. They must be able to detect setups or sting operations by undercover police officers attempting to nab both the contract murderer and client who ordered the kill. Contract killers who don't develop this ability quickly are often caught early in their careers by the police.

In one contract murder that went bad, two killers were hired from the West Coast to go to New Jersey and murder a woman's husband. They arrived in a car that broke down and had out-of-date registration tags. After getting lost, they stopped a passing motorist for directions to the victim's house. The motorist was an off-duty police officer who became suspicious of the men and, upon searching their vehicle, found several weapons and the husband's name, address and physical description written on a coffee-stained piece of paper. These would-be killers did not know how to blend in.

Finding a Killer for Hire

How a killer is found depends, for the most part, on who is trying to find a killer. In many cases—in fact, in the majority of cases—a person looking for a contract murderer has either been in jail herself or has been peripherally involved in crime or frequents the homes and hangouts of known criminals.

If a criminal wants to find someone to "do a job" for her, she puts the word on the street that she's looking. Criminals usually have many contacts within the criminal world. Many of these contacts are formed in prisons. The criminal goes to bars and social gatherings where she knows a strong criminal element will exist. She mentions her search to prostitutes, burglars and robbers, pawnshop owners, cabbies, bartenders and all others who may be of help.

If the murder requires a special tactic or approach, the criminal explains that she needs a good knife man or gunman or fist man. Within this world, contract killers have these types of reputations or specialties. Through these underground criminal contacts, the right person for the job is usually found.

When someone without criminal contacts is searching for a contract killer, he often follows a similar procedure. But because he knows no one within this world, the process is more roundabout. He may first approach a friend or family member with a dark or criminal past and ask her to do the job. If this person needs money, she may agree to do it, depending on her need and experience. If this person has no experience as a killer, she may agree to call "a friend" within the criminal world who knows someone who would commit murder for a price.

But if the noncriminal who is looking for a killer knows no one personally, he goes to the "seedy side of town" and begins asking people who appear to be criminals if they know someone who could do this job. As you can imagine, this can be a frightening search for someone who is probably used to dealing with middle-class suburbanites. But the desperate need to have the intended victim killed usually drives the searcher to take the risk of dealing with the underworld.

Ironically, there is less to fear from the criminals in such cases than from the police. Law enforcement agencies have underground contacts, usually convicted felons anxious to stay on the right side of the law, who report to the police that person X is looking for a contract killer. A law enforcement officer then goes undercover to play a killer. The officer is wired and chooses a meeting place that can be electronically monitored with audio and video recorders. The police need to capture, on tape, person X stating he will pay for a murder. The police also want to tape the exchange of money.

One final risk in hiring someone to perform a contract murder: The killer must be trusted to keep the arrangement a secret after the act has been committed. A murderer probably will not be anxious to confess, but if apprehended, a confession may be made in the hope of a lighter sentence.

Motives

Contract murderers kill again as soon as the money from the last job is spent; after all, it is their way of earning a living. Thus, the time intervals between their crimes generally correspond to the amount of money made from their previous crimes. If the contract murderer made a good haul, there will be a lengthy period before the next murder. But if the killing resulted in a small profit, another will be promptly scheduled.

Elimination Killings

The murder of a person who happens to be "in the way" is called an elimination killing and is the determining factor in a great number of murders. In an elimination killing, the client hires the contract killer to murder someone who has become a threat or a great inconvenience to the client. For example, a client may decide to have a blackmailer killed rather than continue paying out extortion money.

Elimination killings can also be motivated by love. Lovers seeking to remove the spouse that keeps them from being together may hire a contract killer. Or they may decide to try it themselves and save the money. Even if the latter is the case, it falls under the umbrella of contract murder because the killers are doing it for profit, not because of any psychological dysfunction; they are cold-blooded, but not crazy.

In one case, a woman who wanted to get back with her boyfriend left her two children seated in their car seats inside her vehicle and then poured gasoline inside the vehicle, sending both infants to a fiery death. This woman may seem psychotic or to be enacting a crime of passion, but again, she was not acting on the spur of the moment, inflamed by emotions beyond her control. Rather, she killed the children while perfectly rational, in order to elminate what she saw as a barrier to her being reunited with her lover.

Organized Crime

Clients involved with organized crime, vice, gambling and narcotics also order elimination killings. It may be a stool pigeon, a business competitor or the boss himself who needs to be eliminated. Or it may be a disciplinary killing; murder is a regular method of discipline in the underworld.

"Cockeye" Dunn, a notorious waterfront gangster in New York City, testified in his trial for the murder of another waterfront mobster that he could easily order a killing if it was necessary for business. "I would order it like I was ordering a cup of coffee," he said. This method was used when he "had trouble with a person."

Elimination killings among gangsters and other criminals are difficult for police to unravel. If a body is found, the police can usually name several people who would have prospered from eliminating the victim. Since the murderer was a contract killer, however, all the suspects—including the guilty client—will most likely have alibis.

In over 90 percent of these gangland or organized crime murders, the people who order the murders never handle the guns that fire the fatal shots nor drive the cars that are used in the killings. Nevertheless, they are guilty of murder because they hired the killers; on the warrants, the charge would be conspiracy to commit murder. What makes it difficult to convict them is that they will have alibis, proving they were many miles from the scenes of death at the times of the homicides. Unless witnesses come forward, the clients may go free.

There are usually few witnesses to these contract murders and even fewer who are willing to testify. Most know that if the guilty party discovers they are willing to testify, they will be killed. There may even be the threat of murder after the client goes to jail, if his friends are loyal enough to seek revenge. This is the main reason for the federal witness protection program.

The actual killers in contract murders are generally not locals. They are imported from other towns to do the killings and return home as soon as the jobs are completed. To further cloud the waters, they may use vehicles stolen from one part of the city or state, with license plates stolen from other parts. And even if the victim survives and the would-be killer is apprehended, the victim may never have seen the murderer before.

Between 1931 and 1940, the informally organized but tremendously strong confederation of organized mobs throughout the United States employed the killers of what was termed "Murder, Inc." to eliminate sixty-three men in and around New York City. During that same period, they were assigned to about an equal number of out-of-town killings. They went unpunished until one of the lesser members of the mob, "Twitty" Levine, turned State's witness, frightening one of the mob's top men, Abe Reles. Knowing he would be arrested because of Levine's testimony, Reles sought out the district attorney, made a bargain and, in return for promised leniency, informed on the rest of the gang. Reles was later found dead on the sidewalk outside the hotel where the police were "guarding" him. The official police reports said he was "pushed, fell or jumped" from his sixth-floor room.

Contract murderers give homicide investigators a hard time. These investigators may have to wait some time before they can find the member of the gang who will "give up" (identify) the executioners of the gangland or contract murder. When a break does occur, it is not sufficient to just point a finger directly at a suspect. The gang member's word is not enough. The investigators want evidence. But the lead will be followed up, and the new suspect will be evaluated carefully.

Revenge Killings

Revenge contract murders are killings ordered by persons who feel they have been wronged. The father of a ravished young girl swears the death oath. A criminal who has been turned in by a stoolie swears she'll hire somebody to get him.

A fine example of a revenge contract killing occurred in Brooklyn, New York, on February 23, 1952. The body of Steve Bove, a small-time racketeer and ex-convict, was found riddled with bullets near the Gowanus Canal.

In seeking a motive for the murder, police found that on January 9, Bove had been picked up as a suspect in the nonfatal shooting of Carmine Persico. Bove acknowledged that he and Persico "had been" friends, but nothing more. Similarly, Persico claimed to be unable to identify Bove as the attacker. A number of police officers theorized that Persico was biding his time and would exact his private vengeance in the underworld fashion.

Further inquiry revealed that several hours before Bove's body was found, Carmine Persico and his brother were seen talking with Bove on the corner near their homes. They then got into a waiting automobile and were chauffeured to an unknown location. A short while later, shots were heard. The police arrested Persico and charged him with the murder of his former friend, but, of course, Persico had an alibi. He claimed he was with his brother and the chauffeur and was nowhere near the crime scene when it happened, and that was probably true. But he had set up Bove's murder for a certain location and then the contract murderer moved in for the kill.

Jealousy Killings

Contract murderers are sometimes hired for jealousy killings. For example, a woman hires someone to kill her husband's mistress. This is different from a crime-of-passion murder in that the woman does not kill the mistress in the heat of the moment. Rather, she plans the murder and goes to the trouble of hiring a killer. If she kills the mistress herself, she may be able to claim temporary insanity. By hiring the killer, she shows a premeditated conspiracy to commit murder, and it becomes classified as a contract murder.

Killing Out of Conviction

Other types of contract murderers are hired by clients who desire to kill out of conviction. These clients are usually political groups or religious fanatics who wish a person or group of people dead because of their beliefs. The killers may be members of their group rather than outside professionals, and their targets are usually key religious or political figures, such as the leaders of countries, religions or movements. It is their belief that anything, including murder, is permissible because of the importance of their political agenda or the will of their god.

Killers rationalize political crimes involving murder or mass murder on the grounds of conviction. They believe that assassinating presidents or other political figures brings recognition, respect and ultimate victory to their particular cause or movement. Fortunately, murders motivated by conviction are not hidden crimes; the assassin may just walk up to the target and kill him in the broad view of a crowd. Unfortunately, these killers often don't care about innocent bystanders. Car bombs, grenades and other such weapons are used, sometimes with the intention of killing bystanders and spreading terror. These types of contract murderers tend to be unprofessional and unskilled and often are not concerned about being arrested or killed. If they do attempt to evade capture, they leave trails of evidence and are quickly arrested anyway.

Methods

Remember, the goal of a contract murderer is to obtain the reward, whether that reward is furthering of a political agenda or just cold, hard cash. Therefore, the killer uses the method that has the greatest chance of success. The more experienced, professional killer uses methods that vary according to the degree of the job. In other words, a simple target, such as someone who can't pay a loan shark, may warrant a simple kill, perhaps a drive-by shooting or such; whereas a more challenging target, such as a high-level executive with a secure home, bodyguards and such, may require an elaborate sniper setup or a car bomb. The most important thing is that the killer gets the job done and maintains a reputation of competence. If the contract killers do not succeed on their first attempts, they often become the targets of killers themselves and ultimately will be killed for botching the jobs.

Many great detective mysteries involve a contract murderer poisoning the victim, but in reality, poisoning accounts for a minute portion of deaths in any type of murder. It may make for a suspenseful story, but it's not very close to reality.

We have investigated a number of contract murders and are constantly amazed at the different methods used by these murderers. Here are a few methods we've encountered:

- beating the victims to death with fists, gun butts, billy clubs, rocks, cinder blocks, boots with steel tips
- running them over with cars or trucks
- throwing them off of buildings
- pushing them into incinerators
- throwing them into garbage trucks
- locking them in freezers to either smother or freeze
- pushing them in front of oncoming trains or trucks
- throwing them bound off ships at sea in the middle of the night
- setting them on fire
- throwing them down abandoned elevator shafts
- burying them alive

Even this list is pretty abbreviated; professional killers are extremely creative in finding faster, more effective ways of doing their jobs. In one bizarre case, the victim was thrown into a room of starving pit bulls.

The professional level and skill of the contract murderer often falls in line with the actual victim who has to be killed. Let's say, for example, a high-powered executive needs to be eliminated, and the killer the client has hired realizes the job is too big for him. That killer may then subcontract a second contract killer to do the job. The killer the client originally hired thus protects himself from arrest and from becoming a target if he botches the job. It also allows him to establish an alibi, should his deal with the client somehow become known to the police.

The professional contract murderer must know everything about the victim in order to make the cleanest hit possible. The client supplies the killer with photographs and as much other information as possible about the victim. The killer learns the victim's daily schedule; his favorite restaurants; his wife's, mistress's or girlfriend's location; the nights he works late; where he likes to play golf; his exercise routine; and, most importantly, the time when there is some type of vulnerability in the victim's security. After all, even the most important radio, television or movie personality does have some time when he likes to get away on his own. That time is the most vulnerable time for the victim as there is always some loophole or window of opportunity for the murderer to fulfill the contract.

In this particular scenario, the contract murderer often has to follow the victim around, waiting for just the right opportunity. The businessperson may fly from town to town and meeting to meeting, and the contract killer often stays in the same hotel, usually one or two doors away. Of course, the contract murderer has phony identification. This way, if he is later found by the police to be in the same area, he can deny any charges on the grounds of mistaken identity. Many a contract killer has stayed in the same hotel, dined at the same restaurants and attended the same plays or sports functions as the victim to get used to his habits and mannerisms before moving in for the kill.

Most victims of this type seem to be murdered in situations where they least expect to be confronted, while in the bathroom or while quickly returning to their hotel rooms to change clothing, for example. Many times a contract murderer hides in the room or suite where the victim is staying or in a bathroom the murderer knows the victim will most likely use during the course of the evening. Most murders in public restrooms are committed with knives or some other sharp object, as the murderer does not want to attract the attention gunshots would bring. Since most bathrooms are tile, the sound of a shot would reverberate so loudly and attract so much attention that the murderer would likely be caught within seconds of committing the crime. Even guns with noise suppressors are surprisingly loud in a public restroom.

Bizarre Bathroom Killings

In one bizarre case we investigated, a contract murderer went into the stall next to the victim's. He waited for the victim to seat himself comfortably on the throne, then leaned over the wall separating the two stalls and quickly doused his victim with Smirnoff vodka, which leaves a very faint odor. The killer then lit a vodka-soaked towel and threw it onto his victim, igniting and killing him.

Another enterprising bathroom killing took place in a small seashore town. The killer waited for his victim, an executive from New York City who had a summer home at the shore, to use the bathroom at his favorite seafood restaurant. As soon as the victim went into one of the stalls, the contract murderer placed a premade sign on the men's room door that said, "Sorry, out of order." He then placed a bomb outside the victim's stall and quickly left the area. The victim was killed instantly when the bomb exploded. Unfortunately, a six-year-old boy didn't heed the sign on the door and was also killed immediately.

Low-Budget Contract Murderers

When using low-price contract murderers, you often get what you pay for. They generally are not discreet and are therefore prone to being arrested. They get the job done and are no-frills kinds of killers, oftentimes using clubs, bats, sticks or their feet or hands to beat the victim to death. Often the victim's screams attract a lot of attention. Additionally, low-budget killers may have trouble determining if their victims are dead and either beat their heads in or strangle them to make sure. These extra steps take more time and increase the attackers' probability of being arrested. Low-budget murderers stick around the scene much longer than more professional contract murderers would.

Low-paid contract killers are usually rough-and-tumble hoods from poor areas, trying to make names for themselves in the underworld. Their clients are usually middle- or low-income people who want to eliminate middle- or low-income victims. You would not want to send a low-budget killer after a high-power target like the pope or the president. Even wealthy executives are beyond the level of the low-budget killer.

These murderers often accost victims in the street near

the people's homes or in public places. They do not make the elaborate plans the professional contract killer makes, which is another reason they are arrested more often.

We have investigated contract murders where the payment has been as low as $50 and others where the payment was as high as $50,000. The range of payment is as broad as the range of the types of murderers. Some of them are ex-convicts, and most of them have some military or weaponry background. Others are simply bone breakers and goons who will do anything for a buck.

Investigation and Capture

The investigation and capture of a contract killer are probably one of the best examples of just how important confidential informants and street contacts are to the police. In these types of cases, information "on the street" is crucial both before and after "the hit."

It is important to have solid street information and informants *before* the hit to nip the actual hit in the bud. This is done at the point when a person is seeking the services of a contract killer. The police will attempt to set up an undercover officer to play the role of the contract killer. The criminal conversation between the undercover officer and the person hiring the "killer" will be recorded, via either audio- and/or video-tape. This is to corroborate the fact that there was an attempt to kill, and that it wasn't just "a fantasy." This also serves as excellent evidence at trial—there's nothing like the defendant hearing his or her own voice plotting a murder to encourage a guilty plea. Many a husband (or wife), after swearing to the police that they can't believe their spouse plotted to kill them, is flabbergasted when they hear the actual voice of their spouse arranging everything.

The importance of having good street contacts and informants has a lot to do with the speedy response necessary when a threat is received. Police officials do not want the spouse who is trying to set up the hit to go elsewhere . . . such as to a real contract murderer. Although these contacts usually ask for a higher "fee" for divulging this information to the police, the life and death nature of their information commands the higher price.

In cases where the hit has already occurred, and the subject used a contract murderer, informants and good street contacts are again crucial. "Loose lips" have sunk many a contract murderer. Outright bragging and disclosures made under the influences of alcohol and/or crack frequently aid police in the capture of the actual contract murderer. But for this information to reach law enforcement ears, these contacts and informants must first be willing to face the police without fear of being associated as a "snitch." That means that the police *must* take good care of informants if they want to use them in the future. The worst thing a police officer can do is to "burn" an informant (meaning not paying him or her as promised for their information, or revealing to others the informant's status as such). A seasoned detective knows the value of a reliable informant and treats him or her like gold.

Informants come from many walks of life: jail-house snitches looking to shorten their sentence in prison for some information; ordinary citizens who are cop "buffs"; a person the police officer has arrested in the past and now wants to assist the police because the officer treated the ex-con with respect; or persons with access to a lot of information, such as bartenders, barbers, cab drivers and prosititutes, to name a few. These informants are the key to cracking contract murders.

E I G H T

FAMILIAL MURDERS

In this chapter, we'll look at one of the most shocking types of murder: familial murder. This type includes any murder committed within the family structure, such as spousal homicide, parents murdering their children or, just the reverse, children killing their parents.

Familial murders always seem to make front-page headlines in the local newspapers and top stories in the evening news. As we're sure you remember, a few years ago the media overflowed with coverage of Lyle and Erik Menendez, two brothers who were found guilty of murdering their parents. Perhaps our fascination with this type is due to our inability to understand how a person could kill a family member. We are especially shocked when parents kill their children. A public outcry went up several years back when we all heard about a South Carolina woman named Susan Smith who murdered her two young sons.

Familial murders occur more often than many people think. The most common type is spousal homicide. Let's begin with the husband killing his wife, detailing how and why these murders occur.

Spousal Murder: Scenario #1

This husband is a hard worker. He is trying to build a comfortable life for himself and his wife by working as much as he can. He may even work two jobs so he can earn enough money to support his wife and fulfill not only her needs but also her every craving. She is demanding and acquisitive and shows little gratitude for the things he buys her.

The long hours and the pressures of work combined with a lack of relaxation and sleep eventually make our husband irritable, depressed and anxious. He has little time to enjoy with his wife, which creates a problem for both of them. Her needs for sex and romance soon find an outlet when, while shopping for groceries one day, she bumps into an old love. They begin to have an affair.

At first, the old lovers meet only once a week at a local motel. The wife hides her movements with pretenses of doing the weekly grocery shopping. As time progresses, the lovers begin to meet more frequently. The hotel bills begin to grow, so the adulterous pair decide to meet at the wife's house. It's less costly, but, more importantly, if the husband calls, the phone is usually answered, casting little suspicion upon her. But as more time goes by, the wife falls in love with her new partner, and she grows less and less concerned about her husband's feelings and suspicions.

Motives

The husband, at some point, begins to wonder why his wife is behaving so differently toward him. His suspicions increase when a close friend tells him a man has been seen coming and going from the husband's house in the middle of the day. The husband begins to spy on his wife, gathering the evidence he needs to confront her.

He doesn't plan to kill her; he just wants to ask her why

she's having the affair. He is even willing to forgive his wife, hoping the marriage can be saved. But the friend who first reported the affair begins to nag and belittle the husband about the wife's behavior. At this point, his tension levels—already high from overwork—rise even higher.

Once he has enough evidence of the affair, the husband confronts the wife. Though he has planned this confrontation for weeks, and never even considered killing her, the various forces we've outlined come together and the result is spousal murder. A few different scenarios may take place.

Methods

Our husband comes home early from work and sits and waits for his wife's return. He begins to imagine his wife with her new lover. Rage builds inside him. When the wife walks in, she is startled to find him sitting on the living room couch. She asks for an explanation for his early return home, and he asks her where she's been.

At this point, she realizes what is about to happen, and she removes herself from the living room and enters the kitchen on the pretense of putting her groceries away. She is also utilizing these free minutes to conjure up a story she feels will pacify her husband. The husband follows her into the kitchen and continues in a somewhat concerned voice, seeking answers to his questions. The wife may or may not admit at this time where she's been, but at some point, either through the admission of guilt or the evidence already obtained, the truth is brought out. Tension and fear are running high. He feels jealousy and disappointment; she feels afraid of his wrath or relief the secret is finally out.

Whether inspired by fear or relief, the wife suggests a getaway vacation where they can work on the marriage away from any distractions. But he continues his accusations, even plays a cassette tape that he made of her confessing her love for her lover. The wife feels trapped and begins to lash out at her husband, telling him what a lousy lover he is and complaining that he is never home to satisfy her needs. Hearing this, he begins to slap her around, and she screams for help. Fearing that the neighbors will call for the police, he puts his hands over

TIP ══════════════════════════════════

Statistics show that most domestic disputes occur in the kitchen. They might begin in that room or they might not, but for some reason they usually end up there. In the kitchen, of course, there are an assortment of sharp objects that can be used by both the victim and the suspect. The victim may use a knife in self-defense, or the suspect may grab a knife in rage.

Remember, victims of stabbings usually exhibit defense wounds on their hands, forearms, elbows and lower legs. Fingers may be severely cut, even severed. If a blunt object, such as a hammer, is used, hammer marks—small circular bruises and welts—are found in the aforementioned locations.

───

her mouth and she retaliates by kicking and punching him. They are both knocked to the floor, and he is on top.

The hands go from around the mouth to around her neck and he begins to tighten his grip. Not knowing or realizing what is occurring, until she is lifeless, our suspect slowly kills his wife.

In a different scenario, the husband will begin to smack and punch his wife as she screams for help. At this point, he will grab a carving knife off the wall mount and begin to stab his wife repeatedly until she falls or until his rage subsides, even after her death. A large number of stab wounds—ten or more— are not uncommon.

Concealing the Evidence

Often, the suspect will pretend to arrive at his home and uncover the horrible incident. He believes his acting while talking to the 911 operator could win him an Oscar. He pretends to be horrified, confused, shocked. Surely the operator has been moved to tears.

Not likely. His performance is, in fact, his first mistake in trying to conceal the murder. Remember that 911 calls are recorded and can be listened to again and again by police officials. A phony call can be recognized, especially if the slightest errors in tone or information can be heard over and over.

And such errors are impossible to avoid. Imagine yourself

making such a call to cover up a murder. How would it feel? What would you say? What little tricks would you use to deceive the operator and subsequently the police? Now imagine yourself coming home and actually finding a loved one dead, covered in blood, lying on the kitchen floor.

The mind-sets are significantly different. Even a professional actor would have a difficult time sounding like someone who has just found a beloved family member murdered.

If your spouse killer uses a sharp weapon, there is going to be a large amount of bloodstains, which could be analyzed by the police forensic specialist. If the suspect uses a hard object and causes a blunt-force injury, there may or may not be a significant amount of blood to analyze at the scene.

TIP

The writer must remember that with either blunt force or sharp object injuries, the first strike will not be noticeable. That is, there will be no bloodstain. So, if you have one hit or one stab, you will not observe the movement or direction of that assault. When a knife is thrust into the victim's body, the weapon will not collect blood until after the second assault. Therefore, you must always add another strike when you are doing your bloodstain interpretation.

After calling the operator, he looks down at himself and realizes his clothes are blood soaked. He could make the excuse that it's from picking up and holding his wife. Again, this could be disputed through bloodstain analysis. If he decides to abandon his clothes, he may do this prior to calling 911. In any event, his story can easily be either confirmed or disputed.

When writing about his discarding the contaminated clothes, use items located in the house, such as a pillowcase, a trash bag or, let's not forget, a suitcase. Favorite methods of disposal are throwing the bloody evidence off a bridge, digging a hole in a wooded area and burying the bag or burning it in a fireplace or the backyard barbecue.

With any method, remember the time frame. Too often we see mystery fiction in which the disposal is accomplished far too quickly. The killers, many of whom have not planned the murder, think far too clearly and systematically in the world of film, television and novels. In real life, the killer is in a state of shock and confusion. He is terrified by the enormity of the act he has just committed. He may try several disposal methods and locations before choosing the one he feels is best. All of this takes time.

In the cases where the killer decides he wants to remove the body from the present location, he may do this in a variety of ways. He may bring the victim to an easy-to-clean area, such as a basement or a bathroom, and dissect her. By cutting the body into pieces, the killer can more easily move her; it is a lot easier and less conspicuous to place a trash bag in one's vehicle than it is to carry out an entire body.

Investigation and Capture

Forensically, this crime leaves a lot of evidence for our technicians. The device used for the dissection—frequently a hacksaw—can be matched against the separated limbs and the cuts on the body. The technicians examine the size and type of cuts and compare these to the blade. The clothing also contains cuts and tears the technicians can easily compare. The scene itself, no matter how thorough our suspect is in his cleanup, can be easily examined using a number of forensic techniques and applications to collect evidence.

It is not uncommon for our suspect to obtain cuts or bruises during the fight leading to the murder or during the dissection and removal. A smart detective asks the suspect to strip and checks all areas for bruising or other injuries. If wounds are located, they are documented with close-up photography.

In some cases, the murderer is not careful in covering his tracks. Sometimes, once he realizes what just happened, he begins to panic and think of ways to dispose of his victim. There have been times when our suspect contacted the police and confessed to his crime, but more than likely, he will blame the victim for the altercation. Detectives sometimes use this same strategy during the interrogation process to convince the suspect to confess, as in this example:

Police: We understand your wife was cheating on you, and here you are working two jobs so you could buy her that

TIP

Most forensic specialists use 35mm camera systems. This is done for a number of reasons, including the ease of using it, the quality of the photograph and the interchangeable lenses. When photographing an injury, a macro lens or a close-up lens is used because it generates a 1:1 photo, which produces a picture of the injury to the exact size as it is seen.

One photograph is taken with some type of ruler (scale) next to the bruise or cut; another is taken without a ruler. The reason two pictures are taken is that if you just have the photo with the scale, a sharp defense attorney during cross-examination will imply you are attempting to hide something by covering it with the scale.

new car she wanted, and how does she repay you? She goes out and screws around on you. That's how she repays you, and you have every right to do what you did.

The suspect shakes his head up and down in an affirmative motion. He feels that his action was justified and begins his long confession.

Spousal Murder: Scenario #2

Now, let's turn the tables and make the wife our killer. Her husband is verbally and physically abusive to her, and this behavior has gone on for years. As the husband's alcoholism has worsened, his abusive tirades have become more frequent and more violent. The couple has two children, both in college, and the wife is concerned about the financial consequences of a divorce. Nevertheless, she threatens to leave her husband. He swears to change his ways, but the abuse continues. She threatens again, and he responds with a threat of his own: He will kill her if she tries to leave him.

Motives

This woman has several motives for killing her husband. First, his abusive behavior has caused her to hate him. She wants revenge for the beatings he has given her. She also is afraid that if she simply leaves him, he will make good on his threats. Furthermore, she is concerned about how she will support herself and her children if she leaves. But if she kills him, she can live on his life insurance and he will be unable to hurt her or the children. She begins to plan the murder.

Methods

Now, how does she do this? She slowly increases the life insurance policy on her husband by convincing him that if he were to suddenly die, her children would not have any resources to finish their education. Once this is accomplished, she begins to look for someone to commit the murder. The two most common ways are to pay a killer or to befriend a new lover and have him commit the murder.

To find a killer, she begins to go to seedy bars, asking for information or looking for a person willing to perform the execution. This is a mistake commonly made in such scenarios. Her unusual inquiries quickly draw attention to her, and, the next thing you know, she's hiring an undercover cop or a police informant to kill her husband.

A safer, and common alternative, is to approach a friend, acquaintance or family member who is in financial distress and offer to split the insurance money. The risk here, of course, is that the person will report the request to the police. The wife must be certain this person desperately needs the money or has such low morals she would agree to commit murder.

When the deal is struck, a plan is formulated. Friday night is coming and it's customary to go to the local watering hole for dinner and dancing. The wife acts as though nothing has changed; in fact, she's even more affectionate than usual to show others how much she loves her husband. There is dancing and conversation, and everything is rosy. Not a hint is given about what's about to happen. But our suspect has already prearranged a location where she'll have her husband killed.

On the way home, the wife drives, and at the secluded prearranged location, she pulls over, perhaps faking car trouble. Or if the husband knows the killer, she may say, "Look there's cousin Bob. Looks like he needs a ride," and then stop the car.

Once the vehicle has come to its final resting place, the

husband and the wife exit the vehicle and the assault takes place. The killer, who in many cases ends up being the wife herself, shoots the husband once or twice making sure he is dead and then, perhaps, flattens a tire of the car. She fabricates the following scenario for the police:

> We were driving home from such a wonderful evening, not a care in the world, and we got a flat tire. My husband got out to change the tire and a vehicle pulled up from behind with two men wearing ski masks and gloves who proceeded to demand money at gunpoint. My husband wasn't moving fast enough, so they shot him and sped off leaving me holding my husband in my arms until he died.

In another scenario, a wife looking to kill her husband may trick a new lover into committing the murder. We have all read about this happening, especially schoolteachers tricking their students into killing their husbands for them.

A wife may befriend a fellow, and as time progresses, so does their intimacy. When our suspect feels the love is strong enough, she hoodwinks her lover into thinking they need to get rid of the husband. She may reinforce this by injuring herself and telling her lover that her husband is responsible, which will obviously enrage the lover. Now remember, if the lover agrees to do away with the husband, the wife can always say the boyfriend is totally responsible for the killing, and she won't have to worry about location or concealment of the crime or the body. The only concern is disposal of the weapon (if it's hers), which can easily be dropped into a river or lake.

In this scenario, the husband is at home sleeping. The lover enters and shoots the husband while he is lying in bed. The wife's story to the police would go like this:

> We were sleeping and were awakened by a noise. My husband went to investigate, and I heard a shot ring out. At this point, I ran to where the sound came from and I found my husband lying in a pool of blood.

A rear door or window could be jimmied open to make it look like forced entry, as in a burglary. One logistical problem in this scenario is that the victim is lying in bed. His body has to be dragged downstairs and a scene must be fabricated that will fool police forensic experts. How to do this? She can start off by using a small-caliber handgun to minimize any bleeding and quickly remove him from the bed and transport him to his final resting place. But will this really work? Probably not.

When a handgun, no matter the caliber, is fired, there is always a certain amount of trace evidence left behind. This can easily be spotted by a trained detective. So a better scenario is for the woman to wake up her husband, tell him she hears noises downstairs and send him there where the killer is waiting in the shadows.

Investigation and Capture

How would the police counteract this story? By placing some type of electronic device and having the killer talk to the grieving widow while recording her confession of her involvement in the murder. This is not so unusual as it might seem. If the killer fears he will be arrested and sent to jail for murder, he does whatever he can to save himself. And if the wife convinced him to do the murder, he is quick to say the murder was not his idea. He wants her to suffer the consequences along with him—and to possibly lighten those consequences for himself.

In this type of murder, there is often a large body of evidence that the marriage was not good. During interviews, family, friends and co-workers are asked about the nature and quality of the marriage. If circumstances point to the possibility that the spouse had some motive for the murder, the investigators evaluate evidence with that fact in mind.

Parents Who Kill Their Children

Mother dumps baby in garbage can. Father beats child to death.

We've all heard of this type of murder, which is one of the most heinous acts that can be committed. When news of a parent murdering her child is reported, it seems to strike a chord within all of us, especially those of us who are parents. We know how much we love our own children, and therefore we find it difficult to believe that someone could be so cold and ruthless as to kill her own child.

But it happens. In one of the most famous cases of recent years, a woman from South Carolina, Susan Smith, killed her two sons by driving them into a lake, where they drowned. She reported the boys missing, stating that a black man had carjacked her, with the boys in the backseat of the car. She later broke down and admitted she had committed the murders herself.

Motives

In many of these types of cases, a stepparent is the killer. The stepparent may also coerce the parent into committing the murder, perhaps by threatening to end the marriage or simply by pushing the parent to do it. In cases involving preteen children, the parent, often a woman raising the children on her own, commits the act to keep a lover from leaving. Susan Smith falls into this category.

The motive here is one of fear of losing a relationship. This type of murder is carefully planned and executed. Another motive for this type of murder is anger and frustration due to the child's crying and nagging. The parent loses control and simply doesn't realize the child is much weaker and more fragile than an adult. A beating turns into a murder. In this situation, no planning took place. The parent realizes the child is dead and scrambles to hide the evidence. In many cases of this type of murder, alcohol and drug abuse play a major role.

In some cases, a parent kills his spouse along with the children, literally wiping out the entire family. Perhaps the killer feels the family has become a nuisance. Or monetary gain may be the motive. If all the members of the family have life insurance policies, with the killer as the beneficiary, their murders could add up to a lot of money. This motive is especially common when stepparents murder the children and the spouse.

Methods

Methods vary widely in these cases. Some of the most common include:

- suffocating the child, to make the murder seem like a SIDS (Sudden Infant Death Syndrome) death

- dropping the child, especially a very young one, to make the murder seem like an accident
- beating the child, especially with blows to the head
- starving the child
- shaking the child, usually an infant, when the baby won't stop crying
- poisoning the child, often by giving the child cleaning products and household poisons to drink

What should be clear from this list is that the method depends heavily upon the motive. If the murder is done in a fit of uncontrolled rage, beatings and shakings are most common. If the murder is done in a planned, calculated fashion, poisoning, starving and suffocating are most often used.

Since children have limited worlds—only a few friends, limited acquaintances, limited mobility—the parent knows he will be a prime suspect in a murder case. The parent therefore almost always tries to make the murder seem like an accident. The child "fell out of the window," the parent tells the police. The child "was playing with a loaded gun when it went off." Or the old standby, "The child never came home from school," is used in the hope of masking the murder by making it look like a kidnapping. In some cases, especially with teenage children, the parent may try to pass off the murder as a suicide.

Investigation and Capture

This type of murder is easily investigated and solved by the experienced homicide detective, forensic specialist and medical examiner. Nearly all of these cases leave telltale signs quickly discovered in the forensic lab, such as antemortem injuries found on the body. These injuries could be as simple as bruising around the child's wrist, suggesting the child was held by the wrist during the murder.

The detective can discern through questioning whether the murderer is lying. As we mentioned earlier in this chapter, it's tough to accurately pretend you are shocked and horrified about the death of a family member. Since the parent-child relationship is so special, a parent is usually even more distraught than, say, a spouse. The grief creates a particular kind of shock in the parent that not even a great actor can replicate. The detective who is suspicious of the parent's involvement in the death asks probing questions and soon realizes the parent is, in fact, the murderer.

The medical examiner easily locates old injuries that cannot be seen on the surface but are quite obvious in the autopsy. For example, bruises may not be visible on the skin but are easily spotted when an incision is made and the muscle tissue is examined.

Children Who Kill Their Parents

When children kill their parents, it is usually because of some type of physical or verbal abuse. The Menendez brothers, for example, cited numerous abuses to explain why they killed their mother and father. While we don't know if they were telling the truth, we have seen in our own experience a cycle of abuse, usually physical and sexual, in cases of familial murder.

The physical may be the beating of the child's mother by the father, in which case alcohol is generally involved. This type of family environment causes extremely low self-esteem in the child. Living in a hostile, violent environment creates feelings of anxiety and anger in the child. Often the child suppresses these feelings around the parents, with whom he can probably not express them safely. These feelings of anger, anxiety and low self-esteem often lead children and teenagers to drug use and make them especially susceptible to peer pressure.

Motives

These killings, like the spousal killings, mostly occur during stressful altercations. Because the family environment is so fraught with suppressed emotions, the trigger for this altercation could be anything. Remember that this is not a family that communicates well or shows its feelings in constructive ways. The trigger could be as simple as grades on a report card. The parent could express anger or concern about poor grades and something in the child simply snaps.

Remember that a child's reasoning and behavior are different from an adult's. A few years ago, we investigated the suicide of a six-year-old boy who hung himself because he had not received the toy he'd wanted for Christmas. Not getting the toy probably triggered a release of all sorts of pent-up feelings.

So the motive for this type of murder is sometimes more difficult to determine than for one involving an adult suspect. Even the child may not know exactly why he did it. His motive could involve a complex range of emotions, many of which he is not consciously aware.

Methods

Just like in spousal killings, a number of methods and weapons can be used. Since these murders are often unplanned, methods and weapons are chosen for expedience rather than effectiveness. The child picks up whatever is close to him—a kitchen knife, a screwdriver, a letter opener. An older child may kill by physical assault, such as choking the victim to death. A younger child would probably not be strong enough to kill in this way.

One method of killing that we see more often in spousal homicides but may also be used by children is poisoning. Though child-parent murders are traditionally spontaneous, this methodical approach is occuring more frequently. The poison is usually administered over a period of time, beginning, perhaps, with a small dose in morning coffee. Then, as the victim becomes weaker, the child slowly increases the dose, killing the parent.

When a real weapon is used in this type of murder, it is usually a child's hunting or sports weapon, such as a shotgun. The child has easy access to the weapon and is familiar with its characteristics. Also, the weapon is not feared by the intended victims. He can approach them without arousing suspicion.

The scenario surrounding this method of killing the parents would more than likely be while they are asleep and are easy targets. When the child killer is going to kill her siblings as well, she may use a variety of weapons, mainly to camouflage or make as little noise as possible during the killings. This act is thought out over a period of time, and the details are gone over with a fine-tooth comb.

Usually, the child killer uses a blunt-force weapon to kill

any siblings, such as a hammer or a baseball bat. There have also been times when a knife has been used, especially on the younger members of the family since the killer was much stronger physically and could control any resistance.

Once she takes out the children—but remember, this is not always the case—she then moves on to the parents. At this point, she shoots the father first, fearing attempts to suppress the assault, and then proceeds to the mother. She may fire additional shots to make sure the job is finished.

If the child is going to attempt to cover up any of her actions, she may pretend not to remember what happened. She says she blacked out or went into some strange mental state, which could help sustain an insanity plea. Another way out would be to plead self-defense. Or the child killer could claim that an unknown intruder entered the house and committed the deeds. The child may even go as far as staging some type of forced entry to a rear door or window.

Investigation and Capture

These investigations are usually wrapped up quickly. A trained detective will realize from the start that something is wrong. Forensic personnel can easily spot the inconsistencies with the target's statement. The problem lies with getting the target to confess because they must be handled as if they were the victim—that can't be apprehended "full force" in hopes of getting a quick confession. The detectives will treat the target as if *he* is a victim and then confront him slowly with the facts that point to him as the killer.

Sibling Murder

Another familial murder occurs when a child kills a sibling. This type of murder is rare. Most investigators do not see many such cases in their careers. Still, it does happen, so we have included some basic information on the topic. If you choose to include this type of murder in your fiction, be aware of the unusual nature of these cases and know that your investigators would not have worked on a lot of such murders.

Motives

When siblings kill each other, the explanation is often as simple as one child becoming more popular than the other. Perhaps this child feels the attention he is receiving is not as great as he believes he deserves, because his sibling is always in the parental spotlight. Perhaps a brother or sister is particularly successful in school, sports or some other activity, and the killer is jealous of these accomplishments. Sibling rivalry, therefore, is a common motive for this type of murder.

Mental imbalance is another common motive. In this situation, the killer is psychologically disturbed, and the victim dies mostly due to proximity. The sibling is simply nearby when the killer flies into a homicidal rage. The victim's proximity to the killer also provides opportunity. If the deranged killer feels compelled to murder, a sibling is often the easiest victim available. They share a house, sometimes even a bedroom. If the parents are not around, the victim can be killed without much trouble.

Though a younger child sometimes kills an older one who has been abusive over a long period of time, the killer in this type of murder is usually the older child. Often a male child, he is bigger and stronger than his victim and can fool or confuse the victim into following some plan that leads to murder.

Methods

In some cases, the murder is quick, the result of sudden rage in which an older child kills simply because a younger brother or sister is the closest person to the killer. But more often, the murder is planned over a long period of time. These types of homicides can vary. One scenario is the child's taking the victim to a wooded area or other prearranged location where a knife has been strategically placed. Once they arrive, an assault takes place in which the murderer overwhelms his sibling. A friend of the killer may also assist.

Another scenario is even simpler. Two brothers go for a walk through the woods, and when a certain location is reached where the killer feels comfortable, he finds a rock or a large stick and beats his victim to death.

To hide his victim, the child killer may dig a shallow grave. In some cases, he may remove items of clothing from the victim to simulate a possible sexual assault. Or he may just pile some rocks and leaves over the body and walk away.

Now, remember, he has planned this completely and knows exactly what to do next. Mommy knows Johnny left with his little brother, and she expects Johnny to return with him. And when Johnny returns home without his little brother, his worried mother is going to ask a lot of questions.

But Johnny is prepared. He explains that he was walking with his little brother on the way to the grocery store, when a blue four-door sedan pulled up next them. A very large man was inside and motioned for Johnny and his brother to approach his car. When they were near enough, the large man reached out through the window and pulled Johnny's little brother through the window and sped away. Johnny was even sharp enough to get a partial license plate number.

If Johnny has blood on his clothes, he says he tried to save his brother, who was bleeding. If the body of the brother is found, the murder is attributed to the man in the blue sedan.

Investigation and Capture

This is similar to the aforementioned scenario, but the killer's parents must be contended with. They are not going to believe that little Johnny hurt his brother. The detective must maintain the parents' cooperation to get Johnny to talk to him. This is tricky since he has to consider Johnny's constitutional rights. Hopefully, there will be some forensic evidence that can be useful in solving the case.

STRANGER AND FAMILIAR STRANGER MURDERS

Two common types of homicide investigators deal with are the stranger murder and the familiar stranger murder. In the stranger murder, the victim and the murderer are unknown to each other. In the familiar stranger murders, they may be only known to each other by a common bond. They may be neighbors or co-workers who share a nodding acquaintance but not any sort of real relationship.

Stranger Murder

Motives and Methods

In earlier chapters, we discussed a number of murder types that could fall into the category of stranger murders. For example, you know from reading the chapter on street gangs that one gang member may kill a rival gang member for showing disrespect. However, this same gang member may also kill a complete stranger who has no gang affiliation for that same disrespect.

A case in point: Gang members wear an outfit and the outfit shows pride and loyalty, and one achieves the membership and the right to wear "colors" after a long initiation period. Now, let's say our stranger victim is walking down the street wearing his favorite pro ball team's cap and jersey. To our stranger victim, he is just wearing this because he feels a loyalty to his favorite team.

The only problem is that the team colors are the same colors as our street gang member wears. In the gangbanger's mind, the stranger's wearing these colors is a sign of disrespect, so he walks up to the victim and after a very short conversation, in which he may or may not discuss the apparel, our gang member, probably using a semiautomatic pistol, fires a volley of rounds into his victim until he is dead.

This occurs in the daytime, in the evening hours, in the early morning hours, on a deserted street corner or at a crowded bus stop. This street gang member has no fear. While analyzing the crime scene, law enforcement officials may notice that the victim is wearing gang colors, even if accidentally. They may connect these colors to the gang and conclude that this is the motive for the murder.

Stranger murders also occur as a result of arguments begun by motorists in traffic. Motorist A may have cut off motorist B, or driven too fast or too slow or simply in the wrong lane. Gestures are exchanged, horns are blown. Perhaps the two motorists drive next to each other and shout obscenities. Anger turns to rage and rage turns to violence. At the nearest rest stop, gas station or restaurant, the two meet, on purpose or by accident, and motorist B pulls out a gun and ends the argument for good. By the time the police arrive, motorist A has been killed by a complete stranger. Motorist B is long gone.

This type of murder is extremely difficult to solve, because it is so spontaneous and happens so quickly. Usually there is little or no physical evidence left behind, nor are there any eyewitnesses to supply descriptions and clues.

Another example of the stranger murder involves psychopathic killers. These types have severe emotional and mental problems and kill for no explainable reason. They may receive some sort of thrill, as we have discussed in other chapters, or may be following a psychological compulsion they don't question or understand. The choice of victim is more arbitrary than in the first two examples. There has been no perceived act of disrespect or annoyance. The victim is often chosen simply out of convenience.

Mauro witnessed this type of murder in his early teens. While waiting at a subway station, he saw a man pushed onto the tracks just as the train was approaching. The victim died immediately. The killer, a complete stranger to the victim, was not apprehended.

This method of stranger murder is more common than most people realize. Since the murder is so seemingly without motive, finding the murderer is difficult. Witnesses at the scene are so stunned by the suddenness of the crime, they do not attempt to apprehend the murderer and usually cannot even provide useful descriptions.

Wrong Place, Wrong Time

Sometimes the stranger killer is not upset with a stranger victim and is not even aware of the number or identities of her victims. She is angry at someone else—a former employer or lover or a place of business she believes has wronged her in some way. The stranger victim is killed simply because he happens to be at the wrong place at the wrong time.

A common example of this type of stranger murder is the indiscriminate bomber. The bomber, usually male, is most often a loner who, for some unknown reason, decides to place a bomb in a location to kill people. One reason would be the stranger killer is upset with the the local grocer, because he feels the grocer shortchanged or overcharged him. Another possibility is that the killer is upset with the grocer for stocking certain ethnic foods. The killer is angry and anxious about changes in his community, particularly the recent influx of an ethnic group, and he blames the grocer for providing the newcomers with their customary foods.

So the killer retaliates by building a simple explosive de-

TIP

When you are writing any scenario where witnesses are involved, do not feel you have to have all the witnesses agreeing on the same description of the suspect because this never happens. The witnesses are asked to remember the circumstances of the crime and to describe the suspect. The interviewer asks them to repeat their stories over and over again in the hope that more and more details will be added. The witnesses are separated and each are interviewed in this manner. They are asked what they remember seeing. They are then asked to describe the suspect. If the suspect had a weapon, they are asked to describe it. Once this preliminary interviewing is concluded, the detective then asks specific questions in an attempt to obtain even more details.

Some witnesses remember a great deal of information, including a small scar on the suspect's left ear. Others remember absolutely nothing. Still others make up descriptions because either they want to feel important or they feel it is necessary to provide the police with information. There are even people who give a false description just to foil the investigation. When it comes to police ID sketches, which are police artists' renderings of facial features described by witnesses, we have seen them both ways, sketches that are so complete, the police drawings are identical in every way to the suspect, or just the opposite where the drawing in no way resembles the suspect's features.

Even seasoned police officers, when interviewed after a serious incident, give differing stories of what took place. Each officer focused on a particular danger or threat, and this tunnel vision prohibits the officer from having a clear sense of the entire event. Upon gathering information from all of the officers, an experienced interviewer builds a scenario of what took place, piece by piece.

---

vice that is set to go off when an unknowing customer lifts an item from a shelf. The motivation for this may be to strike out at the owner of the grocery store or it may be to kill a consumer of a certain product.

Another stranger murderer is the one who decides to kill herself and others for any number of reasons. This scenario is more than likely planned out over a period of time.

The suicide-murder scheme runs through our killer's mind over and over again until she determines the time is right. Often the killer builds an explosive device for which detonation will be activated by the killer at a preplanned time and place.

The killer picks a location for two reasons:

- to get even
- to prove a point

She picks the location that will harm an establishment (perhaps a former employer or a store that has not satisfied her in some way). Her goal is to cause emotional or financial damage. To accomplish this, she enters the establishment and positions herself at the location she feels the most damage will be done, such as a crowded checkout, then at the precise moment, she yells out her complaints and explodes her bomb.

Bombs, however, are not always used. As we finish this book, the news headlines report that a man from another country went to Florida, legally purchased a handgun, brought it back to a well-known tourist site in a big city and opened fire on the sightseers. At the conclusion of his murder spree, he took his own life. Investigators speculate that the motive was some type of revenge, perhaps against the United States.

A less common method for this killer is product tampering, which, after a few well-publicized cases in the 1980s, has been taken very seriously by all forms of manufacturing. There are few consumer items that are not packaged with tamper-proof packaging. Most products also include a warning that consumers should not purchase the item if the packaging looks as if it has been opened or damaged in some way.

This form of stranger murder has to be the most obscure of all killings—and the most difficult to solve. The killer picks a product for a reason, such as he feels the manufacturer has brought misfortune upon him or he was a fired employee who is looking for revenge upon his ex-employer.

What happens is that the product is purchased and taken home by the killer, who carefully opens the package and adds some type of poison to the product. Then he carefully seals the container and returns the item to another store's shelves. The reason he returns it to a different store from the one where he purchased it is to prevent detection or to penalize that second store.

The last stranger killer is more of a revenge-type killer. This person kills one person or a group of people at an establishment. This type can also include the familiar stranger killer.

An example: A jilted boyfriend discovers his ex-girlfriend is having the time of her life at the local nightclub. He decides to get revenge. Since the revenge is a spontaneous decision, his choice of weapon is limited. If he has a handgun, it will only contain a certain amount of bullets, so the victim's kill ratio will be limited to the number of persons hit and missed at the shooting spree.

Or: The jilted lover obtains an empty plastic gallon milk container, goes to the corner gas station, has it filled with gas by informing the attendant that his vehicle is down the road and has run out of gas, returns to the nightclub and pours a substantial amount of gasoline in the doorway. Now, in major cities, there are a lot of illegal nightclubs that do not comply with fire codes. Most of these clubs only have one way in and one way out and do not adhere to the occupancy codes. So, in this scenario, when the jilted lover ignites the gasoline, he kills his ex-girlfriend and her new boyfriend as well as any number of strangers who happen to be in the nightclub.

Another example of the stranger killer is a murderer who is upset over the noise the nightclub is constantly attracting every evening. The killer decides she can not take it anymore and takes matters into her own hands.

Therefore, she goes into her bedroom closet and removes a semiautomatic, high-capacity handgun. She walks to the nightclub and, once inside, starts firing indiscriminately at the patrons and the workers.

This type of action can take place at just about any location, such as airports, bus terminals, railroad stations, taxi stands, grocery stores, apartment buildings, community centers, playgrounds or movie theaters. The only formula you have to remember is our stranger killer must have some type of grudge that will drive her over the edge and make her lash out at these unsuspecting stranger victims.

Investigation and Capture

In investigating the stranger murder, the police rely heavily on the testimony of eyewitnesses. As we said elsewhere, the stories of eyewitnesses are sometimes contradictory and inaccurate, so these can lead to a number of dead ends and a lot of wasted time.

Another problem with investigating this type of murder is that little or no forensic-type evidence is left at the scene. The killer is usually not around when the explosive device goes off or the innocent consumer dies after taking the poisoned product.

If this type of killer is caught, it is usually because he has bragged about the killings. He may do this in a public place where his claims can be overheard, perhaps by another criminal trying to make a deal with the police to remedy her own problems. The stranger murderer may tell only close friends and family, but someone in this group may be upset enough by the confession to call the police. Without leads of this kind, the killer is very difficult to catch.

Summary

- This murderer is more often male than female.
- The murderer is often angry, for the reasons we discussed above.
- If the murder is sudden, a variety of weapons may be used.
- If the murder is planned, explosive devices are often used.
- Since the murderer has no direct connection to the victim, detectives may have trouble finding the motive.

Familiar Stranger Murders

Motives and Methods

In familiar stranger murders, the killer has some sort of acquaintance with the victim. They live in the same neighborhood or frequent the same store or work near each other. Perhaps they have spoken in the past or simply nod in recognition when they pass each other in the street. But they know little or nothing about each other. The motive for the murder, therefore, often springs from the mind of the murderer, the result of some obsessive delusion.

This delusional aspect separates the familiar stranger killer from the one we discussed in stranger murders. Though the act of murder may be irrational in the stranger murder, its motive usually has some real basis—the angry gang member really does see the colors on the victim; the outraged motorist really has been cut off in traffic; the vengeful bomber really has been fired from his job. The action these killers take is out of proportion to the offense, but their feelings are not completely based on fantasy.

In the familiar stranger murder, the depth of the relationship is usually unreal. In the murderer's mind, the nodding acquaintance grows into a close personal, sometimes romantic, relationship of which the victim is often unaware. The relationship is based on some strong emotion: love or hate or fear or sometimes a mix of all of these emotions.

Scenario: The Love Connection

Let's continue this discussion by using a sample case. An assistant to the super of a high-rise building in a large metropolitan city has a daily routine of sweeping the front of the apartment building.

A male resident of the building has his female assistant occasionally assist him in working out of his apartment. This occurs only once every two to three months. The first time the super's assistant observed this secretary, we will refer to her as Jane, was about a year ago. He was outside sweeping the sidewalks, and as she was passing, she nodded a good afternoon to him.

On a few other occasional meetings, she may or may not have acknowledged him. Our super's assistant, Jim, begins to fantasize about Jane and even carries a small camera to secretly photograph her as she exits the apartment building. Using these pictures, Jim builds a small shrine to her in his apartment, perhaps in a closet that is hidden from normal view.

As time progresses, Jim continues to increase his fantasies, which may or may not be brought on by additional contact with Jane. Jim may secretly enter Jane's employer's apartment, looking for any mementos of her to add to the shrine. These things may be an umbrella, a jacket or other clothing she may have left at the apartment by mistake. Jim may or may not ask her employer about Jane. In an attempt to learn more about her, Jim follows her back to the office and even throughout her daily routines.

The whole time this is occurring, Jim fantasizes that Jane is responding to his affections, that she truly loves him as he does her and they are made to spend eternity with each other.

When we interviewed persons that fit this profile, they informed us that something specific started this fantasy. In one case, the male suspect stated that the appearance of the victim's legs started his fantasies. In another case, the male suspect stated that it was her kind face and smile that reminded him of his mother. And in still another case, the female suspect stated it was the victim's unrequested but needed assistance in carrying groceries from her car into her apartment on a snowy day.

The fantasy Jim is having occurs over a short or a long period of time. Then some event triggers a need for closure. Jane may notice Jim's odd behavior and tell her boss, or she may contact the police. Some states have stalker laws, which would allow for Jim's questioning or even arrest. Not all states have these laws, so be sure to check if the city in which your story is set allows for such a trigger to occur.

These closures are almost always fatal for the victim. Jim, upon release from prison, attempts to win Jane to his side. He may begin by sending her gifts and initiating additional communications with her. If Jane continues to ignore his advances, Jim physically kidnaps her in an attempt to make her see his side of the situation. Remember, this is Jim's fantasy, and he is strongly compelled to see it come true. He will do everything he can to live out his fantasy.

There have been cases where the victim moved from city to city and the murderer followed her. In one case that was highly publicized a short time ago, a TV news anchorwoman was being stalked by a viewer.

Once Jim achieves physical control over Jane, he, first by persuasion, then by physical force, attempts to persuade Jane to love him. When all else fails, he kills Jane to seek revenge and to cover up his criminal behavior.

Jim may hold Jane as a slave locked up in his apartment until he realizes the inevitable. He may kill her utilizing a number of methods, but this is usually performed in a fit of anger during an episode when his fantasy is not going the way he planned it out. Jim physically assaults Jane, perhaps chokes her to death, suffocates her with a pillow, stabs her repeatedly or shoots her.

Jim may or may not dissect Jane's body in an attempt to dispose of her. He may retain some of Jane's apparel or body parts as souvenirs. What you have to remember when you are writing is to put across the true fantasy aspect along with the needs and desires Jim has.

That final scene may remind you of famed serial murderer Jeffrey Dahmer. His fantasy was to have the perfect sex slave zombie. He paid money for sex with young male adults, whom he knew only through the daily neighborhood life. He then performed lobotomies on them.

His experiments included drugging them, so they would comply, or securing them to the bed with ropes and chains. One technique was to drill into their skulls and inject different types of lye, drain cleaners and other liquids in attempts to create zombie sex slaves.

When they died, he dissected them, not only to dispose of the victim bodies in a concealable manner, but also to eat them. It is widely assumed that one of his sickest performances was to take food to work to share with his fellow employees that was made from different body parts of his victims.

Scenario: The Hate Connection

The Jim and Jane scenario, as you may have noticed already, could fit into lust or sexual murders (see chapters eleven and twelve). Now let's talk about the other side of the coin, the hate connection. This is probably the hardest of all homicides to solve because of the lack of an association between the victim and the suspect before the killing.

The killer, for some obscure reason, again through some

fantasy connection, kills one or a group of persons over a negative situation. Let's examine a sample case.

This murderer has been taking his bus for the past two years to and from his place of employment. During this time, on occasion, the bus driver belittled the killer for not having the proper change, for carrying too many packages or for any number of reasons. The whole time this is occurring, the killer is carrying a deep hatred for this bus driver. What makes it additionally disturbing to the murderer is on occasion when he is belittled, other passengers join in the ridicule and laugh at him. The bus driver and the passengers may feel the jokes are harmless, done in the spirit of fun rather than to hurt the guy's feelings.

But these murderers, as mentioned, are psychologically unstable and bring all sorts of repressed anger and obsessive, disordered thinking to any encounter. The bus driver's real or imagined belittlements are enough to trigger vivid fantasies of murder. This killer, through a series of overheard conversations between the bus driver and other passengers, learns the driver's work schedule and perhaps even the location of his home.

Unlike the love-connection type of murder described previously, in the hate connection, there need not be a triggering event. There may be one—a last-straw event that drives the killer to begin implementing his plan—but he may go into action simply when he has amassed enough information to commit the crime.

For example, knowing that this Friday the bus driver will be working a double shift and will be leaving the bus terminal at around 1 A.M., the murderer scouts out, prior to the bus driver's double shift assignment, the location, the lighting, the amount of people and other traffic that may be in the area at that time of night and any other additional information he feels is needed to carry out his plans undetected.

The killer hides in the shadows, waiting for his intended victim to reach a chosen location, where he shoots or stabs him to death. Once this is completed, he flees the scene and disappears, returning to his everyday existence. The detectives investigating the murder will have a very difficult time finding this killer.

Investigation and Capture

When the police investigate homicides, they begin by looking for a common bond between killer and victim. The lack of discernible motive or connection makes a murder tough to solve. This common bond may be a robbery attempt that turned into murder, a love/hate relationship or a disagreement or other motivation that could lead to murder. To help develop a list of suspects, the detectives ask some basic questions:

- Who had reason to kill this victim?

- What was the murderer's motive?

- Who had access to the victim?

- Who knew the victim would be at this place and this time?

In the case of the murdered bus driver, there is really no viewable common bond between the killer and the victim. Interviews with family, friends and co-workers probably do not bring to the surface our killer and his hatred for the bus driver. The driver himself probably never realized the killer had any strong feelings about him. The adversarial relationship existed entirely within the mind of the murderer.

The investigators, however, interview family, friends and co-workers of the victim, along with anyone else who had contact with the victim a short time before the murder. It is not uncommon for the police to set up roadblocks where they pass out informational flyers about the murder and the victim. Rewards are often offered for any information pertaining to the murder.

As you can imagine, such investigations are long and tedious and may take years to close—if they ever do. This type of killer, if he is crafty and careful, may never be caught. The police rely heavily in these cases on mistakes the killer makes. He perhaps leaves some physical evidence at the scene, such as fingerprints, body fluids, trace evidence or footwear impression evidence (a shoe print).

The guilty party may be observed when securing or disposing of the victim or may be found out by some actions performed after the fact, such as bragging about it or continuing to use the same modus operandi over and over again in future murders.

Though killers like Jim, the apartment employee, and the bus rider may not have murdered before their fantasy relationships with Jane and the bus driver, they may do it again if they get away with it once. Their natural tendency toward obsessive behavior and fantasy building can lead them to new victims. If they do continue to find victims, the police can observe a pattern and take the necessary steps to apprehend them. These steps will include stakeouts, surveillance of the dump zones, criminal profiling, decoys or other standards of law enforcement.

So in your crime story, your investigators need some sort of break to solve the case—an eyewitness, a video surveillance camera, publicizing the scene fingerprints (traced through an automatic fingerprint identification system), the killer telling someone. Otherwise, the case will probably go unsolved.

Summary

- The killer has some sort of acquaintance with the victim, but this relationship is often exaggerated and distorted in the killer's mind.
- The popular term "fatal attraction" can be applied to certain types of familiar stranger murders.
- The motive for the murder can be strong (and ungrounded) feelings of love or hate.
- This type of homicide is difficult for investigators to solve, because the victim has no significant relationship to the killer. A suspect list is, therefore, difficult to develop.

T E N

CRIME-OF-PASSION MURDERS

There is a thin line between love and hate, as the song says. There may be an even thinner line between love and violence between persons in love, and when violence occurs, it sometimes results in homicide. This is what we call a "crime-of-passion murder."

One very sad aspect in crimes of passion is that often the police have been called to a location involving the parties many times prior to the murder. In fact, in more than half of these cases, the police have been called to the home at least five times. In the majority of these cases, the murders result from the spouse's attempt at self-defense during a violent argument.

The perpetrators of crime-of-passion murders are quite frequently police officers or other persons who carry firearms routinely. This is an indication that a firearm's readiness and availability serve as a lethal weapon in an argument where the passion is so high that all normal, regular thought patterns are left by the wayside.

Many correctional officers, police officers, federal agents and the like have been the victims of murder with their own weapons, too, as their spouses had found them or thought them to be cheating on them or, in fact, leaving them for other people. The availability of the weapon cannot be overlooked here, and it is almost always the firearm that is the weapon of choice in the crime of passion.

Women Who Kill

Motives

In our experience, women who kill their husbands or lovers are usually women disadvantaged along several dimensions, including a sense of social isolation. These women live in a loosely structured relationship with men and are poorly equipped to succeed in their daily struggle to survive in society. They have few social, educational and personal strengths to help them rise beyond their limited social levels. These women see themselves as victims in a male-dominated world and a society that is structured to be conducive to successful men. They often have no education or a poor education, almost no skills that are marketable and a history of being led and abused by men, and she may be separated from family and friends due to distance or social classes.

Many of these women come from families in which they were abused as children, typically by their fathers. These women later married men who shared similar personality traits with their fathers. In other words, they seek on some subconcious level to marry men who resemble the people who beat them.

There is usually some key element, a last straw, that drives these womem to kill. Two possible elements are the severity of her injuries upon getting beaten and the frequency of abuse, if that is the situation. Another is the man's frequency of intoxication or drug use. Other incitements to a crime-of-passion murder are a husband's forced or threatened sexual acts on the wife, a wife's threats of suicide and a husband's threat to kill.

Women often blame themselves when placed in a situation

of a crime-of-passion murder. Only a small number of women involved in domestic abuse ever resort to homicide as a resolution for what they see as a hopeless position. However, a woman in the social and economic class we previously mentioned will not only be extremely upset about losing the only man in her life, but she may feel this is the only man she will ever have. If he is taken away, she loses her entire future and oftentimes her only source of income, as frequently she is not employed and the only source of income she has is her man.

Most women who confess to these crimes speak about a terror that almost paralyzes their bodies when they find out they are about to be discarded or replaced by younger and more beautiful women. They build up high levels of anger but rarely experience their anger directly. Usually they direct their aggression inward and appear to be passive receivers of their situations, but occasionally the women strike out as a last defense against what seems to be a no-win situation.

Although some women kill their spouses and lovers for other reasons, apparently most do so when they are responding to some form of victim-precipitated attack. Often, these women have histories of long-term abuse at the hands of the men they end up killing. These women usually kill after a series of heated arguments or volatile confrontations with their slightly older partners.

The final argument typically takes place in a bedroom or living room—it could be in a palace or a shack—usually in the early morning hours. These late-night fights sometimes begin as the couple gets ready to go to bed. They're in close proximity and preparing to sleep together, so the fight begins—or continues. Alcohol and narcotics often play a role in these arguments. One or both parties are intoxicated, and the fight grows out of control.

Men Who Kill

Motives

Men who commit crime-of-passion murders have typically been found to be quiet men who want to be accepted by society despite their aggression but are not able to relate to the world around them. They tend to exhibit a great deal of daily stress in their lives. Most men involved in crimes of passion were taught to keep a stiff upper lip in the face of personal adversity. These men also have a great deal of difficulty expressing their emotions and are usually sexually or physically inadequate; therefore, they constantly have feelings of jealousy. Their wives' innocently glancing at or having short chats with other men result in extreme jealousy that slowly bores away at these husbands. One day, when they cannot take it anymore, these men commit murder based on their wives' infidelity, whether real or imagined.

These types of homicide offenders are more apt to have experienced considerable losses throughout their lives. Perhaps their parents died or were separated from them by divorce, abandonment or possibly institutionalization. Later in life, they experience difficulties on the job, they change addresses frequently and often go through many changes in marital status. These stressful events can combine to spark crime-of-passion homicides, usually resulting in the deaths of the people the offenders fear losing the most—their lovers or spouses, children or close friends.

Perhaps it is the men who feel unable to control their lives outside their families that are particularly likely to exert control within their families. When that also fails, they feel forced to kill, seemingly as a last resort to take control.

Males seem to have a stronger predisposition to murder than females, with the ratio being four or five to one. We have noticed through investigations that a lack of schooling, poor economic factors, personality deviations and insanity all serve to lower the threshold for murder. In the case of a crime of passion, however, even the most educated, influential and sophisticated man is devastated and irrational when he realizes the love of his life has either been unfaithful to him or is about to leave him for the last time. When a man in such a state turns to alcohol or drugs for consolation, his threshold for violence lowers and his urge to kill may increase.

Long-lasting periods of stress become an integral part of the compulsion to lash out and kill a lover or spouse. Men often become murderers as a result of prolonged frustration.

We have found the lives of killers to be more stressful than the lives of nonkillers, and the stress was endured over a longer period of time.

Men who kill their wives or lovers are often drug or alcohol abusers and are more frequently given to verbalizing physical threats and exhibiting violent forms of physical behavior than other men. These men are also more likely to have been abused themselves as children, emotionally, physically and sexually. They are more likely to commit sexual violence against their partners than males who are not involved in partner homicide. The crime of passion involving a man or woman who was sexually abused is a combination of a sexual murder and a crime-of-passion murder.

When we delve into an investigation of the circumstances surrounding a crime-of-passion killing, we try to reveal the situation that confronted the murderer. Knowing the characteristics of the typical crime-of-passion offender and matching them up with the characteristics of each suspect often gives us a place to start looking for evidence.

Methods

The methods used by crime-of-passion murderers, for the most part, are not very sophisticated; these murders occur quite quickly and are not usually thought out. One exception to this rule is the murder involving a successful insurance salesman named Robert O. Marshall. Marshall took out an extremely high insurance policy on his wife, planning to kill her. Upon returning home one evening with his wife asleep in the seat next to him, Marshall pulled into a rest area where he had hired men waiting to kill his wife. When he pulled over, the men jumped out of the bushes and shot his wife, leaving Marshall also injured. When the police arrived, Marshall's story was that he had gone over to the rest area because he thought he had a flat, when all of a sudden men jumped out and ambushed them and killed his wife.

The detectives investigating the scene noticed some peculiar characteristics concerning this murder. Number one, it appeared that it had been well planned, since the murderers, according to Marshall himself, were extremely close to where the vehicle was and were armed and ready to kill anyone as soon as the car pulled in. Number two, there was no indication of an attempt to rob either party of jewelry or money. And although Marshall disfigured a tire to make it look like it was going flat, detectives were able to determine the damage was deliberate and could not have been caused while driving, since it did not pull or rupture after being punctured as it would have had it been moving. This is an example of a premeditated crime-of-passion murder, as Marshall desired his wife out of the picture to make room for his new lover. The elaborate planning of the murder resulted in the more serious premeditated murder charge and also a longer prison sentence for Robert Marshall and the killers.

As we said, however, most instances of this type of homicide do not occur this way. The usual circumstances include the husband coming home to find his wife in bed with another man, the homosexual finding his lover in the arms of another person or the wife finding a note in her husband's pocket upon checking out his suit. One of these circumstances, combined with the aforementioned alcohol, stress and pent-up rage results in a crime-of-passion murder.

Weapons

The weapons used in these homicides vary tremendously. Knives, guns, poisons, cars, blunt instruments, asphyxiation, explosives—all of these have been used, as well as the murderer's bare hands. Firearms are almost always readily available, causing some to question how much this availability itself contributes to the incidents of crime-of-passion murder. The waiting period required by almost every state prior to purchasing a firearm is specifically designed to deter those influenced by anger or other strong emotions who wish to kill themselves or others. The waiting period gives them time to cool off and sober up.

Weapons Women Use

One interesting aspect of a crime-of-passion murder concerning men who are murdered by their female spouses or lovers is that in most cases, these men are murdered by their own weapons. The very weapon that has been kept in the home by the male to protect the female from intruders is used against him when the wife or lover is angered. A weapon has been known as a great equalizer, though, a woman using a knife as a murder weapon, as opposed to a gun, exposes herself to a greater risk of successful resistance by her male partner because she must approach him with it at arm's length. Our experience has shown that over 80 percent of women who kill their spouses or male lovers use firearms, with knives being the second weapon of choice.

One method used more frequently than most people would imagine is poison. A respected sergeant in a local town thought for years that his wife was a poor cook. Her cooking made him sick and caused diarrhea and frequent vomiting. After years of complaining, one of his friends began to suspect that perhaps the cooking was more than accidentally bad. Sure enough, samples of the sergeant's hair and nails revealed high traces of arsenic. When the sergeant's wife was arrested and charged with attempted murder, she said she wanted to slowly torture him to death to punish him for years of infidelity. Because of his good looks, women frequently talked to him and sought to be around him. In reality, however, the sergeant had never been unfaithful.

A subsequent background check of his wife revealed that she had been previously married, with her first husband dying of an apparent heart attack on a cruise to the Bahamas. It is suspected that this husband in fact did not die of a heart attack but was most likely poisoned on ship by the sergeant's wife.

Weapons Men Use

Men who kill their lovers during crime-of-passion murders do not show a preference for any one type of weapon. For men, the murder weapon is often the first thing they can find at the scene. This may be a firearm or knife, if one is nearby, or it could some common household item. Here are a few possibilities:

- axe or axe handle
- baseball bat
- board
- bottle
- brick
- candlestick
- cane or crutch

- coatrack
- electrical cord
- fireplace tool
- hammer
- lamp
- piece of pipe
- small table or nightstand
- small television set or radio
- tire iron
- wrench

Most crime-of-passion murders, once again, are quick; they occur in seconds. Therefore, there is little attempt by the suspect to clean up the crime scene. However, if the site of the murder lends itself to the possibility of cleanup, the murderer may try to hide his crime. If the murder occurs in a bedroom and children are present, obviously there is no time for the killer to clean up the scene. However, if the couple is away at a secluded cabin by themselves, the killer has much more time to clean up the crime scene.

In such cases, it is clear to seasoned detectives that the longer a person has with the body before discovery, the greater the chance the murderer will create a staged scene. In other words, he will try to make the homicide look like a burglary or robbery gone bad. The seasoned detective recognizes a staged scene. There is a neatness about such scenes, a logic that true murder scenes do not have.

Investigation and Capture

One clue that tips off detectives immediately that a murder is not strictly a stranger murder but is a crime of passion is the number of wounds inflicted on the victim's body. For example, we have investigated many cases where a spouse or lover was found with dozens and dozens of stab wounds. This indicates there was a relationship between the murderer and the victim of passion. A stranger committing a murder only uses the wounds necessary to disable and murder the victim. However, a crime of passion occurs with much anger, rage and jealousy, and it is the constant stabbing, striking, slashing or shooting that leads detectives to conclude the murderer was in fact related by some strong relationship to the victim.

In one case where Joe was working for the New York City Chief Medical Examiner's Office in Manhattan, there was a middle-aged male, a physician, found on the second floor of an exclusive condo on the West Side. He was found facedown with his face in a jar of margarine, fully disrobed. Upon flipping the body over, it was found that his penis had been skinned by the murderer. The investigating detectives had a hunch he had been killed by a lover during a crime of passion because his lover thought he had been having an affair. Their hunch turned out to be correct.

However, the twist arrived when the arrest was made. His lover was, in fact, another man, and the victim was the recipient of a lover's rage. In this killing, the murderer disfigured the only object he could think of to make the victim no longer cheat on him.

Again, crime-of-passion murders are quick, intense and violent, the result of are all the emotions that are built up in the murderers themselves. The violence is evidenced by the victims' actions immediately prior to their deaths. They almost always have defense wounds on their bodies from fighting off the violent attacks.

Defense wounds are the wounds found on the palms and backs of the hands and forearms caused as a person tried to ward off a blow to the upper body. Defense wounds are found on the body no matter what weapon was used. Even if the weapon cannot be stopped, it is human nature's self-preservation instinct to raise the hand to protect against the blow. Remember for a moment the last time you tripped or fell off a bicycle. As you fell to the ground, you instinctively placed your hands to block the fall. Of course, you realize your hands will get hurt, but this movement wards off any further injuries to your face and upper body.

Therefore, there will almost always be defense wounds on the crime-of-passion victim, if the victim is not surprised. There have been cases where the victim has been surprised while sleeping or by a quick shot, but this is almost never the case as this type of murder involves a violent confrontation usually immediately followed by the murder.

Case Study: Crime of Passion

In a local town in our county, we once investigated a crime of passion that had all the classic elements discussed in this chapter. The husband was an accountant in the town; the wife did not work. Though the accountant's firm was not especially successful, the couple lived in an exclusive neighborhood. The wife was very concerned about keeping up with the Joneses, and, according to the husband's later testimony, she constantly berated him for not making more money. She compared him disparagingly to the other men in the neighborhood who made significantly more money.

The marriage, needless to say, was not a good one. The situation continued to worsen until one day the husband came home from work to find that his wife had bought a $1,500 vacuum cleaner from a door-to-door salesman. The husband flew into a rage. The wife argued that other wives in the neighborhood had bought one, so she felt entitled to one, too. The argument grew out of control. The husband, brandishing a kitchen knife, began chasing his wife around the house, finally catching her in the garage where he stabbed her thirty-seven times.

He then fled to his parents' home in Pennsylvania. From there, he called a few times every day for several days, leaving messages on the answering machine. He always ended the messages by telling her how much he loved and missed her. He even ordered flowers to be sent to his home. By the time the flowers arrived at the house, the wife had been dead for three days. All of this romance, of course, was done to provide the husband with an alibi for the murder.

When he returned from Pennsylvania, he did not go directly to the home. Instead, he went to a neighbor's home and asked that the neighbor accompany him, explaining that he had left messages and had not heard from his wife and he feared something was wrong. He told the neighbor he did not want to walk into the house alone.

Upon walking into the house, they discovered the wife's

body together. The husband felt that discovering the body in this way would surely eliminate him as a suspect in the murder. But remember what we said in chapter one: The victim of a murder usually knows the killer. A seasoned detective begins investigating by focusing on the victim's circle of family, friends and coworkers. Since the wife did not work, this circle was not large.

After a few days, the husband broke down and confessed to the murder. He said he was under so much financial pressure from the wife's spending that when he saw the expensive vacuum cleaner, he simply snapped. The ultimate irony was discovered the day after the husband was arrested. It seems the vacuum cleaner salesman had returned to the home every day that the wife's body lay in the garage. The reason: He had been contacted by the wife, apparently just before the husband came home on the night of the murder, and been told that the vacuum cleaner was too expensive and she wanted to return it. Of course, by the time he came back to get it, she was already the victim of a crime-of-passion murder.

E L E V E N

THRILL/LUST MURDERS

When you hear of a thrill or lust murder, you may believe it to be motivated by love and passion. However, there is an important distinction between thrill or lust murders and sexually related or crime-of-passion homicides. A thrill/lust murder (hereafter called lust murder) is a gross sexual assault committed by a pathological assailant with deep personality defects. The murder itself is characterized by excessive mutilation of the body, and the pattern of mutilation and subsequent movement of the victim's body carries a certain symbolism related to the killer's pathology. You should not write about a lust murder being tied to solely a sexual motive or passion. The lust murderer's crime is unique, and although there may be sexual overtones in the killing, lust murderers show some of the strongest incidence of personality defects and sexual psychopathic characteristics of all types of murderers.

Although the lust killing is a type of sexual murder, the lust killer is a sexual psychopath and, as such, has certain distinct characteristics. If we read the local papers, we realize that the sociopath and psychopath both receive a lot of publicity because of the public's fascination with their motives and methods for killing.

Psychopaths

A psychopath can be generally described as having an antisocial, aggressive and highly impulsive personality. He feels little or no guilt about his antisocial behavior, and he just can't seem to form lasting bonds of affection with either his own or the opposite sex. This leaves him unable to have normal relationships with people, and if he has any friends, he has very few. He may be the type of person who can make a new friend, but over trivial arguments slowly loses that friend and moves onto someone else.

The psychopath is not really crazy but has a severe mental or personality disorder and lacks the ability to feel guilt or empathize with other people who have problems. In general, he is unable to accept any type of love.

Sociopaths

The sociopath, on the other hand, is someone who has been, during the course of his life, stymied in the development of his personality to its fullest. Because of this, his behavior is solely aimed at self-fulfillment, even if it's at the expense of other people and their safety. Sociopaths usually come in contact with the criminal justice system sometime in their lives because of their inability to live by the rules and regulations of a normal society.

You may even know someone that fits this description. He only cares about his own thoughts or feelings and doesn't ever feel much guilt. He may be always fighting the government or the rules and regulations of the local town and just can't seem to take no for an answer. Of course, we're not talking about people fighting for the good of the community or the good of the nation; we're talking about people who couldn't care less about your thoughts or feelings. They are not very social people and are only concerned for themselves.

This type of person exists in every single walk of life. It doesn't matter if you live in the richest neighborhood or the poorest slum; these people are part and parcel of American society. Although their upbringing has forced these psychopaths and sociopaths to become the way they are, it is nonetheless their inability to feel guilt, accept love and empathize with others that makes them the perfect candidates for murderers. As such, they're the perfect candidates to be characters in your next work.

Profile

Before we delve into the actual types of murders that lust murderers commit, let's talk about some common elements of these killers. The "perfect" lust murderer has some superficial charm and a good intellect. In fact, he may even be a member of MENSA. He is unreliable and has a lack of remorse or shame. He probably has a nonexistant sex life and the characteristics of a person who doesn't really follow any plan of life; he just seems to wander from job to job, or neighborhood to neighborhood, without any care for the future. He is untruthful and insincere and possesses a kind of blasé attitude where nothing affects him or really startles or scares him. He fails to learn from experience, and he's incapable of love.

These people rarely commit suicide. Why? Because for someone to commit suicide, he must have deep feelings of depression, anxiety and brooding, and again, the lust murderer doesn't have feelings.

Organized Lust Murderers

There are different types of lust murderers. One type is known as the organized lust murderer. He tends to be a loner by choice; he feels others are not worthy of his friendship. He's a nonsocial person.

This offender is neat and organized in everything he does. His car, his work, his home, his personal appearance, his demeanor—all show the need for order, cleanliness and neatness.

The organized offender is usually characterized by psychiatrists and psychologists as being anal retentive in personality type, somewhat like Felix Unger in his desire for neatness and orderliness. As we said, this type of offender is nonsocial because he chooses to be so, not because people feel he is bizarre. As such, this person is hard to pick out of the general population as being a good candidate for a lust murderer. During the course of his life, this type of murderer believes no one is worth risking friendship with, so he's perfectly happy being on his own. He goes out to restaurants alone, sees movies alone, goes shopping alone and frequently reads a good book as his form of excitement. That is, when he is not killing!

When characterizing your lust murderer, make sure he is highly intelligent, socially adept and at ease in adapting to new situations. These new situations, which are normally upsetting or stress related to the average person, do not affect the organized lust murderer. Also, these types of murderers tend to be, both jobwise and lifewise, very mobile, and they have no need to stay in areas that are familiar to them.

Again, when creating this type of character, give him a true psychopathic personality; that is, he has very little trouble making friends but keeps all his friendships on a superficial level. Did you ever meet a person and, after speaking to him for several minutes, feel you had known him all your life? This is the type of person the organized lust murderer is. One prime example is Ted Bundy. Bundy was so charming and capable of putting a person at ease that, after speaking to him, most interviewers felt as if they had known him for life. It is most likely that this trait makes organized lust murderers able to entice their victims into their own eventual demise.

Motives

Typically, situational stress is what triggers an organized lust murderer's urge to kill. In one case we worked on, a man killed a woman he was dating because while he was out in a restaurant with her, she looked at another guy. This was enough to drive him crazy, and he went emotionally berserk. After he murdered her, he sadistically mutilated her sexually and dismembered her. Although you may say this looks like the work of a disorganized lust killer (see later section in this chapter), remember that it was the stress of her looking at a man that was the motivation for this murder.

Methods

Although the cause was stress, the murder still happened in an organized manner because he took the victim to a particular place, murdered her and then calmly disposed of the body. The amount of stress the normal person would be under in this type of situation would be astronomical, but the organized lust murderer is unaffected.

Unlike the disorganized lust murderer, the organized one uses restraints on the victims and then performs extreme sexual mutilation and dismemberment, as well as crude sexual disfigurement. And again differing from a disorganized killer, an organized lust murderer behaves differently after the murder is committed. For example, this type of murderer often moves the body from the place it was killed to a safe disposal site. This disposal site, unlike that of the disorganized murderer, will not be near where he works or lives.

Disorganized Lust Murderers

The other type of lust murder is the disorganized lust murderer, and he is characterized as asocial because, being disorganized, he tends to be a loner. Other people are very reluctant to become personally involved with him because he is strange or bizarre.

If your lust murderer is disorganized, that has to be his total behavior. His work, home, car, clothing, demeanor and all other aspects of his life reflect his disorganized state. Also, he has a lower than normal IQ, is socially inadequate, lives alone and, usually, is the youngest child of his family. Finally, he generally lives and works near his zone of crime. In fact, if you were to psychologically profile him, he would be a nonathletic, white male, with an introverted personality, who was probably physically and/or emotionally abused in his childhood.

Disorganized lust murderers share several postoffense behaviors. They usually return to the scenes of their crimes, and, strangely enough, sometimes place personal "in memoriam" ads of their victims in local newspapers. Sometimes they change addresses and move, but usually they move within the same neighborhood. They also change jobs after they kill but try to change to jobs in the same neighborhoods as their previous jobs.

TIP

The fact that disorganized lust murders will move, but not far from their original homes, and change jobs, but not far from their original jobs, is one of the few insider tips that experienced homicide detectives will use in tracking down this killer. While the press is printing information about the murderer, the detective is scouring the neighborhood because she knows that the murderer is typically not far away.

Motives and Methods

Let's say your disorganized offender is ready to attack. Does he plan it meticulously? No, he doesn't plan at all because he doesn't have the ability to do so. Also, part of his modus operandi is that he does not usually use restraints on his victim, mostly because the attack is spontaneous and unplanned and the victim is just an object for a sheer act of violence. This type of murderer usually finds victims in the area where both the victim and he live, probably because he feels comfortable only in areas with which he is familiar.

After your disorganized lust murderer makes the kill, what does he do as he stands over the body? Well, he disfigures the face of his victim, mutilates the victim's body and removes the genitalia, which he may take with him. When the homicide detective arrives on the scene, she sees a great show of overkill; that is, the victim has been subjected to extreme violence.

In an example from a case we worked on, a murder was committed involving a meat cleaver. You don't have to have an IQ of 180 to realize that if someone strikes another person with a meat cleaver—even a dull one—a single swift chop to the neck should be enough to kill the person. But with a disorganized lust offender, there will typically be overkill—multiple chops to the head with the meat cleaver, multiple slashes.

Investigation and Capture

As the homicide and crime scene detectives process the scene, they find the disorganized lust offender just as chaotic in his killing as he is in his life, which means there's a lot of physical evidence left behind. Because this type of offender does not appear to be as concerned with neatness as the organized lust murderer, he leaves a lot of clues that help in his apprehension.

TIP

When using this type of character in your work, have the perpetrator:

- leave a lot of blood around

- show signs of no intent to hide the crime or body

- leave the body at the scene (this type of killer won't wrap it and move it to another location)

- perhaps leave a personal effect (a piece of jewelry, a crumpled paper, a cuff link) at the scene (because this killer is unprepared and is acting in haste)

- leave fingerprints (perhaps in the victim's blood)

Other Psychological Distinctions of Lust Murderers

While you are developing your villain, remember that all of these lust murderers have involvement in certain paraphilias. Some common ones are these:

- *exhibitionism*, sexual excitement gained from exposing one's genitals to the view of an unsuspecting stranger

- *fetishism*, the use of a non-living object for sexual stimulation (men may use female undergarments, panties, shoes, corsets and the like)

- *pedophilia*, having sexual activity with prepubescent children

- *sexual masochism*, another chronic disorder in which one derives pleasure from being humiliated, bound, beaten or otherwise made to suffer

- *sexual sadism*, a chronic and progressive disorder in which one inflicts physical or psychological pain on another person in order to obtain one's own sexual excitement

- *transvestism*, a practice in which a heterosexual, typically male, cross-dresses to derive sexual pleasure, may or may not include involvement with the transvestite underground culture or any of the atypical paraphilias, which are listed in the American Psychiatric Association's Diagnostic and Statistical Manual of Mental Disorders (DSM-IV). This includes paraphilias that can't be classified in any other category, such as:
  —*clismaphilia*, sexual attraction to giving or receiving enemas
  —*coprophilia*, sexual attraction to feces
  —*frotteurism*, sexual attraction to rubbing against the genitals of another person
  —*lewdness*, sexual attraction of displaying one's genitalia
  —*mysophilia*, sexual attraction to filth and dirt
  —*necrophilia*, sexual attraction to dead bodies
  —*urophilia*, sexual attraction to urine

- *voyeurism*, looking at people who are unaware they're being watched, catching them naked while changing clothes or, more commonly, while engaging in sexual activity

- *zoophilia*, the use of animals for sexual stimulation, including having intercourse with animals as well as having these animals lick a human's genital area or areas of eroticism

Lust murderers may be involved in more than just some wild sexual practices. They may have a distinct interest in sadism and violence, and in such acts as anthropophagy (cannibalism or vampirism), necrophilia, erotic asphyxiation and piquerism (deriving arousal from the piercing of the body). These murderers are not your typical type of murderer, but have very deep psychological problems driving them to kill. They are the perfect characters to develop long term in your work because they are not the type of randomly violent people who move around the countryside or people who just kill because of being stimulated by sudden anger.

Anthropophagists

Anthropophagists receive sexual gratification from eating human flesh, which is also known as cannibalism, or drinking their victims' blood, which is usually called vampirism. There are many stories of cannibals in recent criminal justice history. For example, Ted Bundy once bit off the nipple of one of his victims and ate it. Albert Fish, who is also mentioned in our chapter on bizarre murders, cooked body parts of several of his victims and ate them. We've found that murderers involved in cannibalism are usually disorganized lust murders. People like Ted Bundy, an organized lust murderer, are exceptions to the rule.

In one case we will never forget, the murderer used a cup to collect the blood from the victim, froze it, and then defrosted it whenever he felt like drinking some. This gave him extreme erotic and sexual gratification, possibly similar to an aphrodisiac. One thing you can explore in your writing is what makes these individuals find sexual gratification in cannibalism or vampirism; that is not very clear. What is clear is that those who start these practices almost always continue to use them. Noting this modus operandi (MO) assists the police in catching them.

Necrophilia

Necrophilia, one of the most bizarre of sexual practices, is usually male oriented, although a few female necrophiliacs are on record. Douglas Clark, aka the Hollywood Strip Killer, was a lust-murdering necrophiliac who allegedly decapitated his female victims and used the heads in sexual acts. Ted Bundy stated during his interviews that he kept one victim, a woman from Utah, for nine days after he killed her. He kept her under his bed, in his closet and then on his bed. He wasn't in a rush to remove her because he knew no one would be coming to his residence. He sexually assaulted her for eight days after her death.

Just as there are different levels of lust murderers, there are also different levels of necrophilia. One level involves only fantasy, in which the sexual eroticism and pleasure are gained by having one's sexual partner pretend to be dead at the time of actual intercourse; there is really no wish to actually have intercourse with a dead body. It is understood between the parties that one sex partner is only playing dead. Prostitutes who cooperate with the police tell of many men who ask them to pretend they are dead. These are usually men of high intellect. They want these women to pretend they're dead as they engage in sexual intercourse but have no reason to want them actually dead.

Another type of necrophiliac is one who has a sexual relationship with someone who is already dead. This person often deliberately places himself in a work situation that gives access to dead bodies, such as a funeral home or morgue, or works as a coroner or medical examiner. This type can almost always be classified as a disorganized offender.

The third, and surely the most dangerous, type of necrophiliac is the necrosadistic murderer. This person kills solely to have sex with a dead corpse. Fortunately, research has shown that very few necrophiliacs are actually of this type, and most of them are willing to just take advantage of situations where they have access to dead bodies.

Some people believe necrophiliacs are feebleminded or have many serious personality defects. In some cases this is true, and in all cases there is evidence of a disturbed personality. But one of the main attractions to this type of behavior seems to be the simple fact that having sex with a corpse means the victim can offer no resistance to the sexual advances of the perpetrator. The killer is excited by the possibility of the sex but not necessarily *because* the partner is dead. And if you are going to create a character who fits this model, remember that the sex act itself is a sort of honeymoon, the culmination of the buildup of sexual excitement.

Pyromania

A pyromaniac is pathologically characterized by a compulsion to set fires and feels sexual compulsion and eroticism by doing so. The act of lighting the match makes him sexually frenzied. Additionally, he becomes so sexually aroused that he has an involuntary orgasm while watching the fire and all of the commotion the firefighters and flames are causing.

As a character in your work, this type of person may

fantasize about women watching a fire. He may stay to watch the women watching the fire, later leaving to masturbate. A sense of power becomes part of his orgasm. This type of lust murderer is attracted to fire, and he is a frequent spectator at fire scenes, though he is often not the actual arsonist.

In the hope of catching this type of lust murderer, the police videotape fire scenes, with the investigators disguised as a television camera crew so spectators will allow themselves to be photographed. The police hope to find the arsonist but also hope to catch persons who are involved in later lust murders.

Trying to understand why pyromania is sexually gratifying is extremely difficult. Although it is usually linked to some sort of stunted sexual development in childhood, sometimes the pyromaniac doesn't start setting fires until he is much older. Asking what has taken so long for this to come to the surface can give you an element to develop throughout your work. Why does your character need fire and sex in his life?

Choosing Victims

In selecting a victim for the lust murderer, remember that the organized killer chooses his victims very carefully while the disorganized killer chooses his victims at random. Also note that most murderers of this type, as well as serial and mass murderers, seem to love the nighttime. That's why many people who are involved in businesses or travel at night are prime candidates, whether they are being selected in advance or whether they just happen to be in the wrong place at the wrong time.

TIP

Waitresses, prostitutes, delivery persons and even police officers—anyone who works late-night shifts—are prime candidates. Of course, the organized lust murderer may very carefully select a victim during the day and then choose to kill the victim at night.

The victim may come in the eye of the organized lust murderer during the day in many ways: a brief encounter during shopping, stopping for gasoline at a station where the murderer shops or works, passing in front of the murderer's car or just simply being observed from afar by the murderer. He may try to get his victim's license plate number, get a name off a luggage tag or listen in on a conversation in a doughnut shop. In all of these cases, people are unaware they are being targeted. A person in front of a lust murderer in the checkout line at the local supermarket may decide to pay by check. The cashier, as part of her protocol for the store, may turn to the innocent victim and say, "May I have your phone number, please?" We have all heard—and done—this. The person tells her phone number, which is mentally recorded by the person in line behind the victim, who just may be a murderer. With this phone number, he scans the cross-reference directories available in the public library and finds the address and name of the person with that number.

In the case of the disorganized lust murderer, all you have to do is be in the wrong place at the wrong time. In one case we worked on, a murderer used a cane to choke his victim to death after she spurned his sexual advances at her place of employment, a small office, when all others were out to lunch. He confessed to us later that he had chosen his victim because she had crossed in front of him while he was walking down the street and he thought she had very nice legs. He calmly followed her into her building, attempted to assault her sexually and, when she resisted, choked her to death by placing the metal cane he was carrying across her neck while pushing her up against the wall. This is a classic case of a person who was innocently going about her own business but was in the wrong place at the wrong time. So the next time you cross in front of a man with a metal cane or give your phone number to a cashier when you're writing a check, be aware of those around you. One of them just may be a lust murderer.

SEXUAL MURDERS

Viewing the victim of a sexual murder is extremely difficult and disturbing, even for the most seasoned detectives and crime scene personnel. Detectives who investigate this type of crime seem to remember each and every detail precisely the way they observed it the day the crime was reported or uncovered. If you speak with these same detectives ten, twenty and even thirty years after the event, they can still relate in perfect detail the scene, their investigation and their interview with the suspect as if the murder just happened.

Detectives handle hundreds of other violent crimes, but the sexual killers seem to be the heartbreakers. In most cases, the victims are young and vulnerable and suffer greatly prior to their deaths. Sexual killings are, in our opinion, the most violent, and the victims the most visually graphic to witness.

The empathy for the victim is far greater for the crime scene detectives and personnel who process the scene than for other investigators involved in the case. A bond is formed between the forensic personnel and the victim because of the time spent with and the closeness to the victim at the scene.

This is also true of the medical examiner at the time of the autopsy. The medical examiner autopsies hundreds of men, women and children who have died for any number of reasons, but the sexual murder victims are the most disturbing.

In today's society, where you can usually find someone willing to perform any type of sexual behavior for a price (or, in many cases, for free), it is hard to believe that these killings still occur. Yet all we have to do to get a taste of criminal deviant society is look at the many reminders we see daily. When we are having our morning coffee, we see the latest statistics of our missing young on the side of the milk carton. As we read the morning newspaper, we undoubtedly come across a story of either sexual abuse or a sexual killing. During our morning commute, we observe at least one billboard for a missing children's hot line. And in the evening, we watch a program dealing with missing or exploited persons.

Sexual homicides are the most complex of all homicides. They can involve one deviant sexual act or an elaborate ritual that is repeated from victim to victim.

Profile

Usually, the sexual predator killer is male. There are few females who kill for sexual reasons. Occasionally, a female helps her male partner obtain the victim or she assists in the actual killing, but to find a female killing for sexual pleasure is very rare.

Motives and Methods

The sexual killer may or may not have been abused as a child, but, in most cases, he experienced some type of sexual abuse that influenced his behavior as he matured. Sexual abuse can be inflicted by one or both of the parents, some other relative, a friend of the family or a stranger.

The sexual perpetrator begins by fantasizing every aspect of the crime, from the initial contact to his last moments with the victim. This includes the way the victim appears. When you have a series of these killings, the victims almost always share common characteristics, such as age, height, appearance and, in some cases, occupation.

When developing your plot, it is important to remember that your victims have to be the most vulnerable society has to offer. Children, both male and female (but statistics tend to favor the female child), and young women are almost always the victims.

A sexual killer has strong compulsions for deviant acts. The only way he can satisfy himself is by having his victim perform exactly as he commands, fulfilling his sexual needs.

The sexual killer shares a lot of characteristics with the serial killer (see chapter on serial murders). Both the sexual and serial killer are on the prowl, looking for vulnerable victims. They secure their victims in the same manner, they may kill in the same manner and they dispose of their victims' bodies in basically the same manner. Like the serial killer, if the sexual killer is left to continue, he kills until he is apprehended.

We have learned from interviewing these individuals that they continue their sexual acts with the victims until they experience a certain feeling of ecstasy. This type of sexual predator refers to this as a mental orgasm. This is not ejaculation, but a feeling of great energy and an emotional release that occurs only in the mind. Some sexual killers refer to this as a rush.

When developing your plot, it is important to remember that your victims have to be the most vulnerable society has to offer. Children, both male and female (but statistics tend to favor the female child), and young women are almost always the victims.

Investigation and Capture

Investigations vary with the incident. Usually with these types of killings, there is more than one victim, so the police will begin by looking at the MO, such as types of victims, method of killing, method of disposing of the bodies, location, where the bodies were disposed of, and will examine any evidence left at the scene. They will then begin to make a profile in an attempt to locate the killer. If warranted, a task force will be formed where a number of detectives will follow up on all leads devel-

TIP

If your killer experiences a mental orgasm, your detectives, medical examiners, forensic personnel and even your forensic laboratory workers may not find semen in, on or near the victim. Not all sexual killers have a physical ejaculation. They may just have a mental orgasm and thus leave no physical evidence.

When there is an ejaculation and the assailant is wearing a condom, the condom lubrication left on the victim can be collected, analyzed and compared for future evidence against him. This is a technique of which few police officers are aware.

---

oped on the case. The police will focus their efforts on stake-outs at dump sites or pick-up sites, and possibly use decoys in an attempt to draw the killer in. Capture will usually result from an unconscious mistake made by the killer or just good police work. When captured, the killer will usually confess to a good interrogator.

Two Common Sexual Killer Profiles

There are basically two general types (what experts refer to as profiles) of sexual murderers. The first is the more intelligent, methodical killer, similar to Ted Bundy. The second is more impulsive and may use a partner in the killings, as did Henry Lee Lucas.

The Ted Bundy Profile

Ted Bundy was a handsome, charming and very deadly sexual killer who terrorized Florida in the 1980s. Bundy was a law student and a Young Republican and often kept his arm in a sling to appear less threatening. Women who stopped to help him with his groceries were abducted, raped and beaten to death. Bundy was executed by the state of Florida in 1989 for the deaths of twenty-two women, but he was believed to have been responsible for even more.

In the Bundy-type profile, the killer usually has above-average intelligence and uses this intelligence as a tool to overcome obstacles. He attracts his victims with his charming personality and good looks, making them feel at ease until he has total control of them.

When he carries out his fantasies, he does so with cool cunning, which will be a great advantage to him because the police tend to key in on the nervous suspect. This type of sexual killer is not distracted by weird fantasies or delusions.

The Bundy-type killer doesn't usually have long-term life goals and is extremely self-centered. Despite his charm and good looks, he does not interact well socially. His only sexual encounters are those of convenience; "love" and "marriage" are not terms in his vocabulary.

The Bundy-type killer shows no shame or remorse for his actions. He is more than likely a loner who feels no one is good enough to become a friend of his.

This killer starts his fantasy with a plan or a strategy about what will occur and may even make contingent plans in case the initial ones are altered.

Because he seeks strangers, he feels a need to become familiar with his victims. He asks a series of well-thought-out questions to become familiar with them.

He attempts to control all aspects of the crime. He demands that the victim speaks, acts and behaves in a certain manner. If the victim is not submissive, the Bundy-type killer becomes very aggressive and demands that she conforms; if she doesn't, he just kills her. In planning for this contingency, the killer brings his weapon or weapons with him.

When he kills, he often uses guns or knives and rarely uses his hands. Because these murders are so well planned, the killer usually has a restraining device ready to use because the act of restraining the victim is part of the fantasy.

When examining the Bundy-type scene, the crime scene technicians find little or no evidence, and there is a good possibility that the actual scene of the crime will never be uncovered. Once the act is completed, the body is removed and placed in a different location than the scene of the crime. This is done primarily to cover up the crime and to distance himself from his victim.

Since this killer is a loner and not likely to have marital

or other such ties, he is extremely capable of moving from one location to another to avoid apprehension. Similarly, he usually acts alone rather than use a partner.

Finally, the Bundy-type killer may keep the victim alive for a time or keep the victim's corpse around, believing there is no rush to dispose of the victim.

Ted Bundy Profile Checklist

- Very intelligent
- Charming personality
- Physically attractive
- Works alone
- Makes detailed plans, with contingencies
- Asks victims a series of questions to become familiar with them
- Controls all aspects of the crime scene
- Prefers to use a ruse rather than physical violence to abduct the victim
- Has weapon when abducting the victim
- Has restraints ready
- Demands victim act in a certain way
- Leaves little evidence at the crime scene
- Removes body from the killing scene

The Henry Lee Lucas Profile

Henry Lee Lucas and Otis Toole traveled the nation's highways looking for victims. Upon finding a suitable candidate, one of the pair controlled the victim while the other took charge of the getaway. After they felt they were a safe distance from the pickup site, they tortured, sexually abused and killed their victim. It is believed Lucas and Toole killed hundreds of people this way. They now await execution in Texas.

The Lucas-type killers were usually reared fatherless or with little contact from their fathers. They almost always had strong matriarchal figures—mothers, grandmothers, aunts—

who took care of them. It is not uncommon for them to have been born into poor or lower-middle-class neighborhoods. Because of low self-esteem and the lack of proper supervision, they are more than likely of below-average intelligence. They are society's outcasts and probably live alone. They have little or no contact with the outside world and frequently move from one low-paying, unskilled job to another.

Another difference between the two types of sexual killers is that the Bundy type is very interested in any postkilling media coverage. For example, he clips articles out of newspapers and videotapes news media coverage. If given a chance, he is more than ready to offer assistance to the media if they request it. The Lucas type hides in fear after committing his murders. He may keep written notes or clippings from a newspaper to assist him in his fantasies and set up altars or discreet hiding areas to secrete his souvenirs. But remorse is quite possible, and he may attempt to seek some type of counseling or religious forgiveness. It is not uncommon for him to return to the crime scene to assure himself he left nothing behind that may link him to his crime.

When this Lucas-type kills, it is usually with little planning; an occurrence of some kind draws his attention and stimulates a response. This could be a beautiful woman walking down the street, a young girl or boy in a vulnerable position or a hitchhiker who looks like an easy victim. He usually does not kill persons with whom he has relationships, but will instead seek strangers. He knows, however, where to find his victims— a local tavern or some such familiar area he frequents or the route he travels to and from work.

There is little or no verbal contact between the Lucas-type killer and his victim before or during the commission of the murder. Since this type of murderer is extremely haphazard, selecting his crime scenes at random and conducting little to no preplanning, the killing is swift and violent and the crime scene technicians will find a fair amount of evidence left behind. Remember, his victims are usually found on the spur of the moment, so he must quickly gain control over them, take them to remote locations and, upon completion of his sexual acts, kill them. There have been many arrests of these types of killers because eyewitnesses or the police themselves observed the murders.

Because of the swiftness of his action, the Lucas-type killer needs no type of restraints to control his victim. More than likely, he commits his sexual acts on his victim after she is dead. Little or no effort is made to cover or conceal the victim's body, and any weapons used are usually left at the scene. These weapons can be sticks, pipes, rocks, boards or, unlike with the Bundy type, the killer's own hands.

Because of the Lucas type's carelessness, foolishness and low intelligence, the police usually have little problem apprehending him, especially if he has a prior criminal record. In addition, if the killer has committed multiple killings, all are easily linked to the suspect because of similarities in the crime scenes. In most cases, the victim's body is not even removed from the initial killing scene.

The Lucas-type sexual killer may take on an assistant if he feels one is necessary. This is usually the case because this type of sexual killer has low self-esteem and feels he needs someone of greater intelligence to assist him.

If the partner is female, the killer may use her to ease the suspicions of an intended victim. For example, if a female hitchhiker is looking for a ride, she is more likely to get into a vehicle with another female present than alone with a male. Or the killer may use his female associate to lure victims to a remote location. Women generally suspect harm more from men than they do from other women, so the female accomplice is often able to bring victims to where the killer waits with less difficulty than if the killer himself attempted it.

In extremely rare cases, the partner assists in the act. In one such case, a young couple was visited at home by a male friend who was recently released from jail. To celebrate his release, the couple decided to throw an impromptu celebration with alcohol and drugs. As the night progressed, all parties involved became highly intoxicated and the newly released acquaintance talked his friend's wife into having sex while her husband was passed out on the couch.

While they were thus engaged, the husband awoke. He began protesting in a loud and violent manner, causing the ex-con to reach into his pants pocket and remove a handgun. With the wife's assistance, the ex-con secured the husband with bathrobe ties and made the husband watch while the other two both enjoyed themselves in front of him.

While this was happening, the two photographed themselves so the husband could have mementos of the evening.

Henry Lee Lucas Profile Checklist

- Below-average intelligence
- Little contact with outside world
- Hides in fear after crime and may feel remorse
- May return to the scene
- Makes no plans, acts on the spur of the moment
- Little or no verbal contact with victim
- Leaves much evidence
- Kills quickly and violently
- Needs no restraints, but often carries restraining equipment
- Uses whatever weapon he finds at the scene (hands if necessary)
- Does not remove body from killing scene
- May have a partner

When the husband again showed his disgust at his wife's behavior, the ex-con shot him. After the murder, the wife and the ex-con continued to have relations. When the time came to remove the victim from the scene, the wife went to the garage, retrieved a saw and, with the assistance of her new lover, proceeded to remove her husband's limbs. Prior to doing this, however, they removed his penis, and the wife began to use it in a sexual fashion while the ex-con took more photographs.

Once the victim was properly dissected and bagged, he was subsequently removed from his apartment and buried in a wooded area. The wife stayed on with her new lover and assisted him in collecting more victims for his sexual killings.

When two male sexual killers work together, things are a

bit different. Rather than lure a victim to a remote location, a male-male team usually snatches the victim with force. One of the men subdues the victim while the other drives them to the murder scene. Often, the two males will have different reasons for killing. Lucas was a necrophiliac, for example, while Toole was more concerned with cannibalism. Their common ground was extreme sadism and a lust for homicide. Their incredibly high body count attests to how well their interests meshed.

Sexual Killer

Let's develop a realistic sexual killer character. We'll call our character Mike.

Mike's sexual deviancy began as a young child when he watched his mother perform sex acts on a number of different male partners throughout his childhood. Mike never knew his father but theorizes he was probably a one-night stand with his mother.

Mike does remember his mother sexually abusing him as a young child and how he felt when this was occurring. Because of this, Mike's victims are female and undoubtedly exhibit many characteristics in common with Mike's mother. These characteristics are not only visual similarities but also may represent the different age ranges in which Mike's most devastating childhood memories of abuse occurred.

To break this down a little further, let's say that Mike's first sexual abuse began when he was five years old and his mother was in her early twenties. Because he is striking out at his mother, his victims are likely around his mother's age.

As Mike grew up, he had no or very few true friends. This was not only because of Mike's dysfunctional personality but also because of his fear that his peers would find out his many secrets. His mother may also have played a part by placing demands on him that didn't allow him to befriend children his own age.

Mike started his violence by taking out his frustrations on a family pet or perhaps stray dogs and cats. This behavior may have begun with hitting or kicking the animals and then progressed to torturing the animals to death. (In one case, we had a young boy setting small animals on fire and watching them run. Later, he would take these small animals and nail them to the inside of his garage door while they were still alive and torture them.)

Mike, as he grew older and more violent, began to collect an array of small but lethal weapons, such as pocketknives, Chinese throwing stars, machetes and BB or pellet guns, eventually advancing to a small-caliber handgun or rifle. In his early teens, Mike began to shoot birds and squirrels with his pellet gun. This is not unusual for teenage boys except that Mike was fantasizing about the killing, the damage the pellet caused and where the pellet entered and left the animal. This was where a mental orgasm began to develop and became a prominent reason for killing.

TIP

If your sexual killer is using prostitutes for his victims, he has to lure them into his vehicle by posing as a john. Therefore, the killer does not wear a mask to hide his identity but may use a mask during the commission of the crime to heighten the fear of the victim and to increase his own excitement.

His cravings to achieve this mental orgasm became stronger and began to develop at this stage. He began to experience that mental release or escape at the completion of his deviant acts. As time went on, Mike progressed from killing small animals to larger ones and, eventually, people.

His needs and cravings are now a driving force in his actions. His nerve is fueled by a desire for the mental or physical orgasm he receives from committing deviant acts and the frustration at not being able to achieve it. Remember, not all sexual killers are looking only for this mental orgasm; there are many sexual killers who are craving the physical orgasm, too.

When he begins to fantasize about fulfilling his sexual desires, he assembles his props to complete his crime. These props relate directly to his fantasy. If his fantasy is to inflict terror, he may assemble clothing to fit the bill. He'll cover his face more to inflict terror than to shield his identity. There are many different rubber and latex masks, but it is not uncommon for the sexual killer to wear a simple ski mask.

If Mike is into sexual sadism, he fantasizes each and every element prior to the initial act. He gathers equipment to use to inflict pain, which can include stripped bare electrical wire to shock and burn his victim. Mike may assemble knives to cut the victim or pliers to rip body parts off. If Mike is into cannibalism, he may ready some type of vessel to carry pieces of the victim's body from the scene. Whatever he needs to fulfill every aspect of his fantasy is ready in advance.

Mike also prepares a room or location that ensures privacy, such as a basement or an upstairs bedroom or attic. He has this location already set up before he seeks his victim. If Mike's fantasy deals with a typical bondage scenario, he has his ropes ready and anchored to a fixed location.

Knots and the way the victim is secured are common traits of a particular murderer and are the same from scene to scene. This is one way the police link each victim to one killer. He may even cover the victim's eyes and place a gag, which could be as elaborate as a ball on a rope or as simple as a dirty handkerchief stuffed down her throat.

It is not uncommon for Mike to photograph, audiotape or videotape the sequence of events, in order to relive his encounter over and over again. Mike may also take a souvenir to help relive his precious moments. These souvenirs can be anything from jewelry and clothing to body parts, such as nipples and vaginas.

TIP

Souvenir gathering is a common trait among sexual killers because they love to relive the killing. When they are unable to get victims, these souvenirs assist them in suppressing and relieving their desires. When the police search the killers' residences, they usually find these souvenirs along with the newspaper clippings about the killings.

Symbolism

A big part of Mike's enjoyment is what some law enforcement experts refer to as symbolism. Symbolism means there is something special, or symbolic, about each of Mike's victims. It may be an article of clothing, the way the victim walks or the color of her hair. Something about the victim attracts Mike's attention.

Often, the victims of a sexual killer fit a certain stereotype. One might be the girl-next-door type; another may be the schoolteacher type. In Mike's case, the victim will be the stereotype most similar to his mother. These stereotypes all play an important role in the fantasies Mike is having. The victim's similarity to a stereotype may be triggered by some symbolic object rather than similarity in appearance. A ring or a necklace may remind the killer of the stereotype, and this similarity will be enough to make the victim suitable. One killer we investigated was attracted by the victim's perfume, which he admitted reminded him of his mother's perfume.

Another aspect of symbolism concerns the victim's body. Mike may be focusing on the private areas of her body. He might take delight in carving the woman's breasts off, or maybe just the nipples. We have seen victims who have been assaulted with sticks or pipes in both the vagina and anus. These areas have been ripped apart in such a manner that these injuries alone could have been fatal to them.

Mike may even carve or burn a symbol or words into his victim. One reason for this may be an attempt to tell the police that he is the one responsible for the killing, a signature. The killer's reasoning here is the same as when he mails letters to the newspaper: He wants to get credit for his work.

Mike may continue with this behavior from victim to victim, or he may change from victim to victim. The change may occur for a number of reasons: the lack of suitable victims fitting his profile or more violent fantasies and the increased confidence to carry them out. Sometimes the victim brings about the change through her actions during the initial stages and directly preceding her death. Mike may be fantasizing about killing his mother, but the girl may say or do something that reminds him of someone he knew in high school. He may then alter his fantasy to one of killing the high school girl. The degree of change, if any, will depend upon how far into the process the shift of stereotype occurs.

Ritualistic Behavior

We are all creatures of habit in everything we do. When we drive to work, we normally take the same route and use the same mode of transportation to get there. If something is successful, we continue to use the same method until something causes us to change it. Even our sexual behavior follows a pattern of habit.

In Mike's case, we can refer to this as his ritualistic behavior. Mike has a certain way of preparing his room and gathering the supplies needed to accomplish his goals. This includes materials needed to secure his victim, like rope, duct tape, chains or handcuffs.

Part of this ritual is the way in which Mike prepares himself prior to locating his victims. Mike showers and dresses in a normal fashion so as not to draw attention to himself. He drives a normal, plain-colored vehicle so it fits into the surroundings.

Mike locates his victims by traveling to the seedy areas of the largest cities nearest his hometown. His victims are prostitutes because he knows they are on the low end of the social scale and feels that police will not try as hard to locate them once they are reported missing. Mike knows that most prostitutes are drug abusers who have little or no contact with their family members, so a missing persons report is unlikely to be filed promptly, if at all.

Mike, once he finds his victim, drives over to her and propositions her as any john would. She thinks she is going with a customer and does not have any idea what is happening. It is common for our victim to be driven to a secluded area to perform her job; therefore, no resistance is given until Mike begins his ritual.

Once he feels he's safe, he may use a disabling substance like Mace or pepper spray to control her. The Mace is used to gain control of her swiftly if she resists so that little attention is drawn to them. Once this is accomplished, Mike uses rope, duct tape, handcuffs, bike chains or any other binding material to gain complete control over his victim. This behavior is carried out from victim to victim in an almost identical form.

Mike transports the victim to his prearranged location and begins to act out his sexual fantasy. Mike likes to have his victims show extreme fear, and he likes them to perform for him. He tells them what to say, how to act and even what to wear. He remembers a certain type of nightwear his mother wore when she abused him and makes his victims wear a similar garment. Mike also remembers the words and how his mother performed prior to the actual sex acts. Mike makes his victims perform in a similar manner.

If the victim does not cooperate the way Mike demands, he ends his fantasy and just kills her, leaving him totally frustrated and ready to locate another victim.

If the victim complies with all his demands, the role play continues until Mike is content. This may last minutes, hours, days or even weeks.

Once Mike feels the urge to kill his victim, he does so while having or immediately after having sexual intercourse with her. He may even have sexual intercourse with the victim after she is dead and continue to do this for days after the murder.

As we said earlier, Mike may have his mental orgasm, and this may be enough for him, or he can have a combination of sexual encounters with his victim. These encounters can include sodomy, oral sex and even intercourse with different parts of her body or penetration inside a wound he created.

Disposing of the Evidence

Once the victim fulfills all of Mike's fantasies and desires, he disposes of her. Sexual killers do this in a variety of ways. John Wayne Gacy kept of most of his victims under the crawl space of his home. Ted Bundy disposed of his bodies in secluded areas or left them in their own residences. In our case, Mike places his victims in various rural areas of his county.

Mike usually follows a pattern because he is comfortable with it. He uses the rural areas because he feels the victims' bodies will not be uncovered very quickly. By the time his victims are found, they will usually be skeletons, making identification very difficult. With other sexual killers, their methods of disposal vary. They follow paths with which they are comfortable and which they feel will not lead the police to them.

Mike is so cautious he removes the victim's head, hands and feet and disposes of them in a different location from the body in an attempt to avoid identification of the victim. Mike uses a large butcher knife and hacksaw to accomplish this task.

Once the dissection is complete, he uses large plastic leaf bags to carry away the different body parts. Mike has a floor drain in his basement, which he uses to dispose of the victim's bodily fluids.

Mike only takes away one or two sections of the victim's body at a time. He feels these small packages are less likely to be uncovered. Some sexual killers drive around with the victims' bodies in the vehicle. Some experts feel this is because of an inner need or desire to get apprehended.

When Mike is at the secluded location, he exits his vehicle, digs a shallow grave, places the victim in it, covers her with dirt and leaves the area. Some sexual killers may put the victims' body parts in dumpsters. Either way, the sexual killer who is rational enough to scatter the evidence will take great care in covering up any and all clues that link him to the victim. Mike makes sure his crime scenes are devoid of clues by wearing gloves, making sure he has no previous physical contact with his victims and carefully disposing of the body. In addition, the sexual killer often has a working knowledge of law enforcement procedures. He may even be an auxiliary or special police officer, and if he isn't, he is more than likely a police buff.

MASS MURDERS

Mass murders occur when several victims are killed within hours or even moments of each other. In many of these cases, an armed person walks into a restaurant, shopping mall, government office or other such public place and begins randomly shooting innocent bystanders. In April of 1990, for example, a man who had been released only one day from a psychiatric institution went into a mall in Atlanta, Georgia, and began shooting everyone in his way.

In recent years, there has been a growing number of cases where a parent or sibling kills an entire family. Additionally, there have been many cases in which people have gone into schools and playgrounds, armed with semi- or fully automatic weapons and shot everyone, including the children.

While there has not been a tremendous amount of research on these crimes, mass murderers do share certain characteristic traits and habits. The killers are usually white males. From our experience, this type of murderer tends to have a low-paying, semi-skilled job, usually involving shift work or other routine-type tasks.

Profile

In most cases, there is a particular victim whom has been selected to be murdered, such as an ex-wife, a former boss, a friend. But the killer, when he begins the actual process of the murder, such as entering the building where the victim is located, opens fire on whomever is in the area.

Sometimes, however, a person feels overwhelmed and frustrated by a perceived injustice in his life and simply shoots victims who, although not directly related to the killer, represent what he is mentally fighting against. For example, if a man is fired from a job a week after being arrested for an utterly unrelated matter, he may feel the police caused him to be fired. In the killer's mind, the arresting police officer came between him and success, so now anyone in a uniform, most particularly a police officer, is his target.

Characteristics

Although their motivations vary from case to case, mass murderers do share some characteristics that may become reasons for the mass murders. Generally, these traits are severe depression, delusional psychosis, violent changes of temperament, alcoholism and the use of pornography.

One telltale sign of depression is mood swings. The person suffering from depression may be extremely happy and energetic one minute and angry or sobbing the next. These rapid changes may occur within a day, an hour or few minutes, and are usually set off by something to which the reaction seems extreme. For example, the person may be joking around and accidentally spill some water on the floor, at which point he becomes extremely angry, curses vehemently and smashes the glass against the wall.

Lack of interest in what's going on around them is another indication of people's depression. They become bored with their jobs, their friends, their significant others and sometimes life itself. They don't want to leave their homes or their bedrooms, they wear the same clothes day after day and they often neglect personal hygiene. Mass murder may be a way of alleviating this boredom.

Similar to their general lack of interest, depressed persons may exhibit a lack of appetite that lasts for weeks. They may eat only their favorite foods or sweets, but even those may become unappetizing to them after a few days.

The mass murderer may also exhibit psychotic behavior, having delusions and losing touch with reality. This may be caused by an organic brain disorder, such as a chemical imbalance or a brain tumor, that impairs his ability for rational thought. Or he could simply be psychopathic, with no sense of his moral or societal obligations. The psychopathic killer is a delusional killer who does not believe what he is doing is wrong.

Mass murderers tend to have violent changes of temperament. For example, a mild, meek person may suddenly become lividly irate and aggressive once certain trigger mechanisms are set off. This often happens because the person has feelings of inadequacy or feels he is being duped by society once again. Michael Douglas's character in the movie *Falling Down* typifies this type of personality.

Also, mass murderers often have problems with alcohol abuse. Although it cannot be implied that alcohol causes people to become mass murderers, there is a high rate of alcoholism among these killers. And alcohol does aggravate the symptoms of depression.

There is also a high incidence of pornography being involved in mass murders. Although pornography may not play a major role in the crime itself, it is one of the higher ranking similarities between mass murderers and serial murderers. Police raids of these killers' homes have often revealed many pornographic videotapes and magazines. Again, as with alcoholism, this does not mean an interest in pornography makes one a mass murderer, but it is nonetheless a common characteristic of these killers.

Motive: Stress

There are some mass murders that appear to be premeditated, as in the case of a Mr. Charles Whitman, who shot at unsuspecting victims from the famous bell tower at the University of Texas in Austin. Whitman carried boxes full of supplies, including food and ammunition, to the top of the bell tower in preparation for his attack on the innocents. Whitman's crime seems to have been motivated by stress, which is why people under great amounts of stress now joke about "going up to the top of the bell tower."

At the opposite end of the spectrum, some cases of multiple murders involve killers whose fury was ignited by a trivial remark, a minor insult or a small provocation. Whether brought on by extreme prolonged stress or an offhand remark, however, multiple-victim murderers do so in an effort to regain some degree of control and pleasure in their lives. To the observer, this motivation may not appear rational, but to the killer, it makes perfect sense, given his psychological dysfunction.

Motive: Hatred of Society

Mass murderers often develop a hatred of society, leading to strong feelings of rejection and failure and the anxiety of not being able to survive on their own. These feelings create frustrations for this murderer that inevitably overwhelm him and motivate him to strike back. For many killers, the best way to lash out against a cold, dark society is to destroy its children. Killing children in a school yard provides the mass murderer with not only a much needed sense of power and control but also a way of taking vengeance where it hurts the community the most. Many of these crimes occur in communities with many schools, shopping malls, office buildings and other such crowded forums.

Methods

The mass murderer often believes that killing innocent people will correct all the wrongs in his life. Since this usually occurs to the killer in a sudden epiphany, he does not usually plan the crime months in advance. Once he does decide to commit the crime, however, he often gathers together more than enough equipment to do the job. In other words, the mass murderer quite frequently has boxes and boxes of ammunition and several semiautomatic or automatic weapons to use to kill suddenly and swiftly. (In one famous case, the killer had enough ammunition to reload his semiautomatic weapons at least 150 times.

Unlike a serial murderer, who will have enough only to kill the victim and perhaps one or two people at a scene, the mass murderer is prepared to take out as many people as is required to regain his place in the world. He realizes subconsciously that this most likely is his last moment of glory, and he wants to go out with a "bang." A mass murderer almost never runs out of ammunition or is foiled by a jammed weapon.

This is not to say, however, that all mass murderers are this prepared. There are certainly cases on record in which the killers used only one or two guns and gave up or killed themselves after shooting six or seven people.

Investigation and Capture

Unlike serial killers, the mass murderer seems to give very little thought to his possible capture or death. In fact, many are killed by the police during the attack, while many others kill themselves once they have completed the massacres. In some cases, the offenders surrender to the police and offer no resistance. It is almost as if they are finally at peace knowing they have committed the murders and, they hope, righted all the wrongs in their lives.

In cases where families are murdered, the killer usually leaves many, many pieces of evidence that will lead to his arrest. Perhaps because he has killed his loved ones, the familial mass murderer may on some level want to be caught.

F O U R T E E N

SERIAL MURDERS

Serial murder is the crime of the 1990s, but is it really new? The term is certainly of recent vintage, having been coined around 1980 to differentiate between mass murders and the more methodical killings of those who spin out their crimes over time. In a report from the National Institute of Justice published in 1988, serial murder was defined in the following way:

> A series of three or more murders, committed as separate events, usually, but not always, by one offender acting alone. The crimes may occur over a period of time ranging from hours to years. Quite often the motivation is psychological, and the offender's behavior and the physical evidence observed at the crime scene will reflect sadistic, sexual overtones.

The phrase "committed as separate events" means that a certain amount of time must pass between the murders. No specific time period has ever been stated, but if only a few hours separate the murders, the killer probably will not be considered a serial killer.

Though serial murder is a worldwide phenomenon, North America claims 76 percent of the world's serial murders. The United States must claim an ignominious 74 percent. Europe runs a distant second with 19 percent. Europe's leaders are England (36 percent), Germany (29 percent) and France (11 percent). The formerly Communist Eastern European nations contribute a mere 1.8 percent of the total, with ten cases recorded since 1917, a fact explained by both cultural differences and the tendency of state-owned media to "lose" bad news.

Although most people believe serial murderers are some new phenomenon, you can actually trace their roots back to the early fifteenth century in France. There was a nobleman by the name of Gilles de Rais who was known for his violent attacks of innocent children whom he would rape, torture and eventually kill. Historians believe that he committed these crimes on at least eight hundred children.

Serial murders extended to nineteenth-century England with one of the most famous serial killers of all time, Jack the Ripper. Jack the Ripper, as you recall, went around the streets of London killing prostitutes. His name became a household word as many newspapers printed Jack the Ripper's story as it evolved.

Throughout the early and middle twentieth century, an occasional killer attracted media attention, such as Charlie Starkweather in the late 1950s, but it wasn't until the 1970s that such killers began to surface with alarming frequency. Our society as a whole entered an era of increased violence that's continued the past twenty-five years. And our awareness of this violence, and of serial killers, increased because television brought these stories into our homes every night.

Newspapers and magazines, competing with television for our attention, gave greater coverage to stories of violence and murder, increasing our awareness even more. This intensive coverage had an ironic side effect: It turned most serial murderers into cult heroes. They were given nicknames, such as the

Freeway Strangler, the Boston Strangler, the Son of Sam, the Zodiac Killer and the Hillside Strangler.

This romanticized view of serial killers has led to their frequent use in mystery and crime fiction. So in this chapter, we will examine some of the common types of serial murders, looking closely at their motivations and how they perform their tasks in real life.

Serial Murders vs. Mass Murders

The terms "mass murderer" and "serial killer" are often used interchangebly in the media. Although they do share a few common traits, the truth is that serial killers and mass murderers are very different. The mass murderer is one who kills a large group of people at one time usually using one device, such as a bomb, or an arsonist who ignites a nightclub filled with people (see chapter thirteen). A serial killer usually commits one murder (sometimes more) at a time over a period of time, which could be days, weeks, months or even years. And the serial killer is one who honestly believes what he is doing is normal and acceptable. To our knowledge, no serial killers kill, then stop; the murders continue throughout the course of a serial killer's lifetime. The only time the slayings actually stop is when the killer is apprehended and placed in jail where he doesn't have access to his victims.

In the case of the famous Zodiac Killer from California, the murders appeared to have stopped, but a suspect was never apprehended. It could be that the suspect was incarcerated for only one murder and was never linked to the others, or perhaps was imprisoned for other crimes. In 1997, a man was arrested in New York City for killing his sister. Some investigators believe this man is the Zodiac Killer, but he has never been charged with any of the Zodiac murders.

Yet another possibility is that the Zodiac Killer may have become incapacitated because of an accident or illness or may have died without the story ever being told to law enforcement authorities. While we don't usually associate these kind of life circumstances with murderers, these things happen to them just as they happen to everyone.

Characteristics: Mass Murderers vs. Serial Killers

Mass Murderer

- Kills a group of people at once
- Drive to kill satisfied after one mass murder
- Deranged individual who explodes due to extreme stress
- Commits suicide or turns himself over to police at end of crime; makes no attempt to escape or hide his crime
- Has no pattern or ritual to his killing
- Takes many weapons and an enormous amount of ammunition to the crime scene
- Is usually male
- Rarely has the opportunity to commit a second mass murder; does not usually become a serial killer
- Kills in order to gain a brief moment of control by controlling the fate of others

Serial Killers

- Kills people one at a time
- Lust for murder must be satisfied over and over again
- Psychotic individual who kills for pleasure ("mental orgasm")
- Employs elaborate techniques to avoid detection and apprehension; will kill for weeks, months or even years until caught
- Has very defined patterns and rituals which he uses in each killing
- Takes only one or two weapons to the crime scene
- Is usually male
- Rarely commits mass murder; prefers to kill one at a time
- Kills in order to gain a brief moment of control by controlling the fate of another

As you can see, there are few similarities, so calling a mass murderer a serial killer (or vice versa) in your work is a glaring error for which many of your readers will take you to task.

Serial Killers

Since so many myths and legends exist about serial killers, let's identify some known facts:

- Eighty-five percent of American serial killers are male; 8 percent are female. Sex remains undetermined in another 7 percent of the cases in which the killers are still at large.
- Eighty-two percent of American serial killers are white; 15 percent are black; 2.5 percent are Hispanic. Native Americans and Asians figure in one case each, with the Asian killer serving as an accomplice to a white male.
- Most serial killers range in age from twenty-two to fifty.
- Surprisingly few serial killers are legally insane. All are cunning, indicated by the fact that more than 18 percent of the cases of serial murder in this century remain unsolved.
- Eighty-seven percent of American serial killers are loners; 10 percent hunt in pairs or packs; 59 percent are from all-male groups (ranging from two-man teams to gangs of a dozen or more), while 23 percent are male-female couples and 18 percent include mixed groups of varying sizes.

Geographically Stable vs. Transient Serial Killers

Some serial killers kill in one geographical location and are therefore known as *geographically stable serial killers*. This type doesn't hunt and roam beyond his immediate surroundings; instead, the killer tries to lure victims into his home or car. Famous serial killers Jeffrey Dahmer and John Wayne Gacy fall into this category, as would Atlanta killer Wayne Williams, who patrolled the streets looking for his victims. It has been reported that trace evidence (such as fibers) from Williams's home was found on clothes the victims wore prior to their murders. This suggests the victims had been in Williams's home before Williams commited the murders.

This type of serial killer usually seeks victims that share

some similarity, such as age or hair color or social standing. The killer, for example, may seek only young, blonde-haired boys or middle-aged, dark-haired women as his victims. Criminal psychologists believe this similarity usually connects to some childhood experience. The victims, for example, may look like the killer's mother or like a special childhood friend.

This type of serial killer is the easiest type to catch because of these two patterns: The victims all live or work in an area near the killer's home, and the victims share some trait or similarity. These patterns allow the police to narrow the focus of the search and locate the killer. Thus, the friends, co-workers and relatives are crucial persons to be interviewed by police as they hold the key to the victim's actions.

TIP

Whether geographically stable or transient, serial killers seem to love to drive. In a significant number of cases, part of the killer's profile was a propensity for driving, usually at night. Some killers go on long drives to find victims far enough away from their homes to avoid suspicion. Others, as we mentioned, cruise their neighborhoods in search of victims. Car of choice? Most often, a Volkswagen.

Geographically stable serial killers can also be loners, living at home with their mothers and sisters, or come from a dysfunctional family. They may seek their victims during the evening hours. These types of serial killers mainly kill prostitutes. Now, most prostitutes have no family contact. They are often drug abusers and are on the lowest end of the social ladder. Since prostitutes are usually runaways, no one really knows their whereabouts—or that they're missing, so their deaths are unlikely to be reported in a timely manner. Clues will probably be destroyed, leaving the likelihood of catching this type of serial killer next to none.

These victims are usually found in remote locations by hunters, years after they've been killed. We can refer back to the killings in the Green River area of Washington State where a number of prostitutes from the Seattle area were found in various conditions of decomposition, mostly skeletal remains.

But the problem with investigating serial killers is that they kill and then transport the victims to other locations, so one is hard pressed to find any type of clues or evidence from a remote dumping area.

The other type of serial killer is the *geographically transient serial killer*. This type moves from location to location, usually to keep his identity unknown. He stays in one location until he feels the police are getting close to him. Most serial killers of this type kill or seek a victim just a short time after moving to a new location. Famous serial killer Ted Bundy (see page 151), for example, began killing less than two weeks after he moved from Louisville, Kentucky, to Tallahassee, Florida. Most law enforcement officials believe Bundy was responsible for an additional thirty-six unsolved murder cases. But some people believe Bundy actually killed more than three hundred young women throughout the United States.

This could be true. Because murderers of this type are frequently on the move, they're more difficult to catch than those who stay close to home. They therefore remain free to continue killing. One serial killer of this type was the most prolific one on record: Henry Lee Lucas (see page 153). When he was finally caught, he admitted to killing more than 365 people.

When this serial killer is apprehended, he may or may not cooperate with the police. It has been our finding that these killers cooperate with the police when there's a deal to be made or if they are of low social standing and education.

Psychological Profiles

Serial killers come from all walks of life. They can be rich or poor, old or young, a loner or a socialite. John Wayne Gacy was a well-known politician and a professional businessman whose claim to fame was how nice he was to children. He even dressed up as a clown and went to hospitals and other locations to entertain children. He was liked by many, and it was quite a surprise when the police found in the crawl space underneath his house the bodies of thirty-three young men.

As with any type of human behavior, serial murder can have many motivations. The same motivations that inspire this behavior in some people could inspire other people to different, even constructive, behavior. But motivation is a cornerstone of the FBI's psychological profile. We will describe the major types of serial murderers, examining the motives that seem to dominate each type. It is important to note, however, that many serial killers have more than one profile, so we can't commit ourselves to writing just one profile for each serial killer in all cases. In actuality, the more victims a serial killer murders, the more narrowly we are able to define exactly what type of killer he is. This is because the type of victim often reveals the type of killer. The FBI creates a psychological profile and constantly hones it with each and every murder the serial killer commits.

Delusional Serial Murderers

Many serial murderers are not considered to be psychologically impaired. They are in touch with the real world but have absolutely no feelings for other people. The opposite of that would be the delusional killer who murders because he has seen or heard people or voices that demand he kill a certain type of person or persons. The new breed of police officers would consider these killers psychotic or psychologically impaired; the old school of police officers would simply call them nuts. There is little doubt about the mental state of these serial killers. In psychiatric terms, they would qualify as psychotic.

But are they really as psychotic as they appear? The rationale behind this question: A smart defense attorney would certainly make the case that their delusions make them good candidates to plead insanity.

Motives

David Berkowitz, the "Son of Sam" murderer, is a perfect example of this type of murderer. When interviewed by the police, he said he heard his neighbor's dog speak to him and tell him to kill. Other delusional serial murderers hear a disembodied voice or see a vision, perhaps of a demon, Satan or maybe even God. Harvey Carignan, who was convicted of murdering six women, claimed that God told him to kill. Carignan also had a distaste for women because he thought they were bad, and he declared he was God's savior put on this earth to do away with all the evil in the world.

Another serial killer was a young boy who decapitated an elderly woman and then stabbed her more than two hundred times. Within the next several weeks, he killed several other elderly women by stabbing them in the upper body. Three other elderly women escaped him, though all suffered stabbings. When caught by the police, he informed them that he was possessed by a red demon that stated he must kill in this manner and that the only pleasure he could possibly receive was killing the way he did. In these last two instances, both killers heard voices in their heads, and they both killed because of their delusions. One set of murders was predicated by God, the other by demons—completely opposite ends of the spectrum.

TIP

Most law enforcement officers, especially the old-timers, may find these delusion excuses hard to believe. They feel these people just kill for the sheer pleasure of killing; they don't really hear voices. The newer police officers, who are trained in psychological behavior, may take a different view on this.

Methods

The delusional serial killer's crime scene is in total disarray. There are probably signs of forced entry, and the scene shows signs of a struggle, such as the victim attempting to flee. The victim is brutally assaulted with either a knife or a club or even both. The victim's body is not carved up, but is stabbed, shot or bludgeoned, not once but numerous times.

When the delusional serial killer goes out looking for his victim, he has an idea he wants to kill but doesn't have a particular person targeted. Experts say there is just something in the killer's mind that clicks before he goes out looking for a victim. When this happens, the victim may be the first person the killer sees or the first person with whom he feels comfortable. Then he attempts to either enter someone's house or apprehend someone from a sidewalk, usually by force, and takes the victim to a secluded area to beat or stab to death.

To aid in abducting the victim, the murderer may use some type of restraining device, such as duct tape or handcuffs, or she may use Mace or pepper spray to overcome the victim. These details are thought out prior to the actual abduction or break-in, which usually occur during early morning hours. We will go into more detail toward the end of the chapter about just how this type of killer operates.

Goal-Oriented Serial Killers

The goal-oriented serial killer wants to achieve some result from his murders. He may want to eliminate from the world people he perceives as worthless. He typically frequents local hangouts or nightclubs, especially places where women congregate. These women, if provocatively dressed, may unwittingly become victims. Killing provocatively dressed prostitutes is one of the most common themes in serial murders by men, as these killers are obsessed with ridding the world of sexual misconduct.

The serial murderer of this type, when confronted by the police, may actually be proud of the fact that he has made the world a better place by eliminating the lower echelons of society, such as prostitutes, streetwalkers or promiscuous women (promiscuous men in the case of homosexual murders). He believes he should be branded a hero, not a murderer, by the police.

Motives

The goal-oriented serial killer has an obsessive-compulsive mind-set and may have deep-rooted psychosexual problems, but he is not delusional. This type of killer does not hear voices or see visions directing him to kill certain types of people; he simply has in his mind the desire to rid the world of a certain group of people who, as classified in his mind, are undesirable and unworthy to live and work with other people.

Methods

The crime scenes of the goal-oriented serial killer vary from case to case. No two are exactly alike. But through the years, investigators have detected a few patterns. This type of murderer usually does his killings at remote locations, and the victims' bodies are not discovered until years later. And rarely does he murder in one location and then dump the body somewhere else later.

TIP

If your goal-oriented serial killer is apprehended by the police, make him appear to be an upstanding citizen: a social worker, a volunteer at the senior citizens' home, the fellow on the block who always shovels the snow for the elderly neighbors, a police buff, an auxiliary police officer, a first aider or, quite possibly, even a police officer. These are the actual profiles of serial murderers of this type who have been apprehended by the police since the beginning of time.

Domineering Serial Killers

This killer actually enjoys seeing his victim suffer. He likes to inspire fear. He gets more enjoyment from the victim's fear, from feeling a sense of control and power over another human being, than he does from the actual killing. Ted Bundy is a good example of this type of killer.

This murderer does not suffer from delusions, visions or voices. He is totally aware of what he is doing and may be very well versed in the laws and penal codes of his area. He chooses, however, to completely ignore the law. He is aware of reality and of the consequences of his action but makes a conscious choice to take a life.

Motives

By having complete control of a victim's life, the domineering serial killer experiences extreme pleasure in making the victim totally helpless and having her do whatever he wishes. After all, this is something that has been done to the killer over the years. He can only experience the other side of this while killing another person.

With the domineering serial killer who first rapes his victims, it is not the sexual gratification the killer enjoys, but actually his use of power and control to dominate the victims, who are quite helpless in his clutches.

TIP

Serial killers tend to be unmarried, possibly living with their parents and, if so, possess domineering mothers and passive fathers. Additionally, they may be meek in personality and have been dominated throughout their lives. As such, they do not have positions of power or authority in any jobs they have but instead are delegated to lower-echelon jobs with no supervisory capacities, such as a janitor or gas station attendant. Actually, they may just live off the social security or other income of their parents.

The domineering serial killer's background may include a unique childhood or adolescence. Possibly, he was someone without a father figure, or someone who has never had anyone respect him in his life. In dominating and killing, this murderer experiences brief moments of glory. For once in his life, he dominates another person.

Let's break this down even further. He may rape his victim or perform some kind of sexual perversion on his victim but not for sexual gratification; he is doing this to strike fear, and it's the fear that becomes his sexual gratification. This is known to law enforcement authorities because the few victims that have survived attacks by serial killers of this nature have told the police that their attackers did not appear to be sexually aroused until the victims became almost "slavelike" persons under the killers' control, forced to follow their every command.

Methods

A domineering serial killer uses what is known in the law enforcement community as signatures—unique ways a person commits a crime, such as removing the victim's head and placing it in a location where the police will immediately see it upon entering. This is done to taunt and torment the police, increasing the killer's sense of power and control.

Sexually Obedient Serial Killers

The sexually obedient serial killer is one who was probably born out of wedlock or whose parents were divorced when he was very young. He is emotionally immature and was probably physically and/or sexually abused as a young child. A lot of these serial killers also abuse narcotics and/or alcohol. He may start out killing small animals, such as cats and dogs, increasing his violent behavior to afflict humans as his sexual fantasies become truer to life.

Motives

This type, unlike the goal-oriented serial killer, kills for the sexual pleasure he derives from his killings.

Methods

The sexually obedient serial killer sexually abuses his victims, whether male or female. In doing this, he uses some type of binding and mutilates the breasts or genital areas of his victims. In one case we remember, the killer actually carved out the woman's breasts. One killer just cut out the woman's nipples, and another actually carved out or cut off the genitalia of his victims.

The sexually obedient serial killer's crimes are very violent and savage, and upon searching his home, one is likely to find all types of domineering and S & M (sadism and masochism) equipment and pornographic material.

Thrill-Seeking Serial Killers

Police respond to a crime scene. They find a woman's breasts removed. Additional mutilation of the body is noted.

Another scene in another city. A homeless man is found in an alley. His genitalia have been removed and placed near the scene. His body is mutilated. Are these types of murderers goal oriented? Are they sexual in nature? Apparently not. They are the work of the thrill-seeking serial killer.

Most thrill-seeking murderers are highly intelligent, and the ones who are not possess excellent street smarts. These killers usually move around quite a bit, making it difficult for police to apprehend them.

Motives

Interviews with serial killers of this type reveal that they commit murder for the sheer thrill of doing it. They describe the feeling of plunging a knife into a body as the most exciting experience they have had in their lives. The cutting off of the genitalia or removal of breasts seems to be fixated sexually; however, it should be noted that the thrill-seeking serial murderers are solely excited by the actual rush incurred by inflicting harm. They kill because they enjoy it and because the thrill is an end in itself.

Methods

This type of killer usually likes to kill with his bare hands, or with knives or other implements that make contact with the body. Thrill-seeking serial killers almost never utilize firearms because there is no thrill: The thrill is associated with the fact that there is physical contact between the victim and the killer.

Although thrill-seeking serial murders include sexual deviance, necrophilia, dismemberment and other types of bizarre methods of murder, remember that the murderers are motivated by the sheer thrill alone and not by any type of real sexual gratification. Although sexual evidence may be found at a scene, as mentioned earlier, this should not confuse the experienced police detective in tracking down this type of murderer.

TIP

Not all serial killers use a weapon to murder their victims. If you look again at Ted Bundy, he pretended he was hurt. He even went far as placing a bogus cast on his arm and soliciting the help of unsuspecting do-gooders. Once they were near his vehicle, he forced the victims into the car. Then examine the case of Wayne Williams the Atlanta serial killer. Notice that he befriended his young victims in such a way that they were comfortable with taking a ride with him. Some of his victims were actually mentally challenged, which made it even easier. Most serial killers are smart enough to realize they will get caught if their victims put up a fight or call attention to themselves, so they actually go out of their way to locate easy victims.

Case Study: Jeffrey Dahmer

One of the most infamous serial murderers of all times is Jeffrey Lionel Dahmer. On July 22, 1991, two Milwaukee police officers observed a man running down an avenue in the city's poorly developed district. They noticed he was in handcuffs as he was running down the block, waving in an attempt to make them stop. He informed the police that his name was Tracy Edwards and he was running from the apartment of Jeffrey L. Dahmer, a person who, for the last five hours, had terrorized and threatened to kill Edwards and eat his heart out. He told the police that he escaped and that he was desperately in need of help.

He accompanied the police officers to Dahmer's apartment, and while there, the police were amazed at what they found. Inside the apartment, they found human remains, including skulls in the freezer and parts of bodies thrown about, and photographs of dead men who had either been mutilated or completely dismembered.

Dahmer, a shy, retiring man, had been arrested by the Milwaukee Police Department on several occasions prior to this for disorderly conduct, for molesting children and for assault. He suddenly became the focus of international notoriety as the gruesome nature of his crimes came to the attention of local law enforcement. A psychological profile of Jeffrey Dahmer revealed he was an insecure alcohol abuser who spent many of his years growing up in a rural area and was deeply affected by his parents' bad marriage. His mother, Joyce, was considered mentally unstable by many neighbors and friends, and after the divorce, she moved to Fresno, California, where she works for a government agency.

In school, Dahmer did not fit the norms and was described by many dates as a likely candidate for killing himself. While his classmates had always seen him as the type to commit suicide, they never considered him violent or dangerous. He joined the military in 1978 and was stationed as a medic in West Germany from 1979 until his discharge in 1981. There, he was recalled to have had incredible drinking binges, drinking until he passed out. On the weekends, he was known to drink all day, pass out, wake up and start drinking again. He had his music playing and seemed to be in a world only known to him. Some weekends, he was reported missing from the base, and when news of the Milwaukee murders came to light, an investigation was conducted by the German police authorities to see if Dahmer was involved in any of several unsolved homicides there.

Dahmer worked for many employers, usually in low positions. He worked for the Ambrosia Chocolate Company as a night worker, but his work habits were constantly under suspicion as he was found sleeping in the lunchroom and was always late. He was also found guilty in 1987 of immoral conduct after urinating publicly in front of several children, but he was put on only one year probation. Years later, an Illinois man informed the authorities that Dahmer had injected him with drugs and stolen his money and jewelry, but that case was eventually dropped due to lack of evidence.

In 1988, he lured a thirteen-year-old boy into his apartment by offering him fifty dollars to pose for a photograph. Dahmer then drugged the child's coffee and molested him before the boy was able to escape. As fate would have it, the boy was the brother of a future victim of Jeffrey Dahmer. Dahmer was arrested and charged with sexual assault and enticement of a child for immoral purposes, and it was judged, in the opinion of the court, that the possibility that Dahmer could be treated and become a stable person in the community was extremely unlikely. Although the prosecutor pushed for a five- or six-year prison term, it was the viewpoint of the judge presiding over the case that Dahmer would benefit more from psychological treatment if he remained outside the prison because the prison did not offer special programs for sex offenders. Dahmer then served a one-year sentence in a correction facility on a work release program that allowed him to continue work at the Ambrosia Chocolate Company.

A profile of Dahmer revealed that he typically found his victims in gay bars, shopping malls or areas of a city frequented by homosexuals. He often lured young men to his apartment on the pretext of watching videos or paying them to pose for photographs. On each occasion after getting these victims to enter his residence, he then attempted to drug, strangle and dismember them. It is also believed by police that, on at least one occasion, he had sex with a dead body. When neighbors in the building complained of the stench coming from his apartment, Dahmer told the neighbors it was simply rotting meat in the refrigerator. He was even known to buy many boxes of Pine Sol, according to the neighbors, as if he were going to try and get rid of the stench, but he always told them it didn't help.

In February of 1992, Jeffrey L. Dahmer was sentenced to fifteen life terms in prison for his crimes. He himself was murdered in prison by a fellow inmate on November 28, 1994.

This serial murder case affected people all over the country. It seemed to bring to light the growing trend of serial murders in all major cities. It is also a classic example of how the quiet, unassuming person is suddenly revealed as a psychopathic murderer.

F I F T E E N

VEHICULAR MURDERS

Vehicular homicide is the real "heavyweight" of murders. Somehow, murder by stabbing, shooting or strangulation seems like small potatoes when compared to the horror of being chased down by a two-ton vehicle, headlights flashing and horn honking, traveling at least 75 mph.

Vehicular homicide is rare because of the size of the weapon involved, be it a car, van, truck or even motorcycle. It is likely to be seen by several people who can identify the vehicle, the physical description of the driver (usually a man who makes no attempt to disguise himself) or the license plate information. It is worth noting, however, that perpetrators of vehicular homicide (if they are smart criminals) try to use license plates that do not correspond to the actual vehicle in use.

Running Down the Victim

The most common way for this type of murder to occur is for the victim to be run over or struck by the vehicle by surprise.

This is usually done while the victim is entering or exiting her home or place of business, either in the early morning or the late evening. The reasons for this are obvious: The vehicle and the person driving it cannot be easily identified.

Hired Drivers

In many cases of this type, the murderer is hired. What usually happens is that a person looking for someone to commit this type of homicide seeks a criminal, but that criminal is almost always of a low-level stature. It may be a teenager who is hoping to step up in his criminal element by doing this type of murder. Or it may be done by some low-level soldier in organized crime who is hoping to move up in the hierarchy.

The person selected does not need any experience or finesse. All he needs to do is operate a vehicle and have some information on the victim. In some cases we've investigated, the person or organization doing the hiring locates a vehicle for the perpetrator. It is the killer's responsibility to dispose of the vehicle, which is usually done by leaving it in a poor section of town where it can be stripped quickly, thus avoiding good fingerprint or trace evidence detection.

This killer will not be highly compensated, certainly not as much as an experienced hit man. We have never heard of someone getting more than a thousand dollars for this type of murder. We once heard of a suspect who bragged that when he was in the lower tier of organized crime, he was involved in doing "rim jobs," meaning that he killed or injured people who owed his organization money. He called them rim jobs because he said he knew he had connected when he felt the bones of the victim snap beneath the rims of his tires.

Motives

There can be many motives for vehicular homicide. We have investigated cases involving contract killings where a person was killed for hire, elimination killings where a person (a wife, a husband, a lover, a business partner) had to be killed and revenge-type murders where a driver is cut off in traffic and reacts by stalking and later killing the other driver while she is leaving her vehicle or home.

Another motive for vehicular murder is jealousy, where

the perpetrator (the lover or enraged spouse) wishes to eliminate the person who is creating the lovers' triangle. Since this killer is often of the middle class, he doesn't own weapons and has not often engaged in violent behavior. He doesn't want a face-to-face confrontation and feels incapable of stabbing someone to death. The car makes the murder seem less direct.

We have also investigated cases where ex-convicts are released from jail only to hunt down the police officers who put them behind bars, killing them as they approach their vehicles while leaving or coming home. In one such case, the police officer was killed as he departed his personal vehicle and walked to the police precinct where he was due to report for the midnight to eight o'clock shift.

So, as you can see, vehicular homicide, although not used too often by seasoned murderers, appears to be deliberately planned. Of course, there are instances where vehicular homicide is committed by a person who is under the influence of alcohol or drugs. And although these are typically defined under state laws as vehicular homicide, they are not actually premeditated murders and are therefore not covered under this chapter dealing with preplanned vehicular homicides. It is worth noting that vehicular homicides do not involve theft or robbery because, as noted earlier, the murderer does not stop her vehicle at all during the commission of the crime.

Methods

Consider this scenario: A man has been contracted to kill Susie Jones as she exits her vehicle after parking it in front of her home at approximately 12:30 A.M. Jones has just come off the four to midnight shift at the local 7-11. She locks her doors and walks slowly across the street, fumbling for the keys to her front door.

Suddenly, a car turns the corner. With tires screeching, headlights glaring and acceleration up to speeds of 70 to 80 mph, it does not appear to be stopping. Jones turns and is immediately blinded by the glare of the headlights. The driver bears down on her, and she goes flying like a rag doll into the air, fifty to one hundred feet, as the vehicle roars away. The killer, confident no one has seen him, drives home and secures his vehicle in the garage. He knows he will be paid handsomely for a job well done.

But, did he really carry out the homicide in such a way that he won't be caught? Did he drive at high speed without applying the brakes before hitting Susie Jones? If he had hit the brakes, the tires would have screeched and skidded, possibly causing neighbors to look out their windows and witness the actual impact. Did he drive with his brights on so as to distract the victim (or anyone else seeing his approach) and prevent her from getting a good look at his face as he struck her?

Did he make sure that, after striking her, he only slowed down a little so as to round a curve or get accessibility onto a major road, thereby not attracting any further attention? Did he make sure to stop calmly at stop signs or red lights, possibly merging into traffic or turning right on red to avoid waiting at a light? The contract murderer would be sure to employ all these tactics in a "successful" vehicular homicide.

Some vehicles are stolen "to order" for this particular type of murder, since it is easier for the murderer not to have the vehicle in his possession shortly after the murder. Following the homicide, the vehicle is driven to a clandestine location where it may be dismantled totally and slowly sold for scrap or crushed and discarded in landfills. Many of these murderers use older vehicles that are dispensable and not worth much money so they can be discarded after the murders.

The marks that may be left at the scene, such as skid marks, tire marks, dirt from impact, blood tissue and hair, chipped flakes of paint and broken equipment such as trim or headlights, are frequently clues for the detective to catch the murderer. Keep in mind, though, that this type of murderer never stops at the scene of the accident to collect this evidence. He continues on and takes a chance on the police not matching the actual vehicle to the murder scene.

In a particularly violent accident, bloodstains and tissue may also be found on the radiator, the door handles and other parts of the vehicle, such as the grill and headlights. When the accident takes place on a dirt road, particles of soil may adhere to the fenders and the tires. If the chemical composition of the soil is characteristic of a particular location, it may be possible for the detectives to associate the vehicle with the scene of the accident. A suspect vehicle will be placed on a service station jack so a highly trained detective can study the understructure for various clues, such as impressions in the grease or the fibers, blood and tissue of the victim. So if the killer wants to avoid suspicion, he usually travels hours away from the scene, sometimes into another state, to have any physical damage to the car repaired.

It is also common for these murderers to go through car washes ten to twelve times, usually in many different locations so as to not cause suspicion by visiting the same one a dozen times. However, a large majority of these murderers wash their cars at self-service car washes where they can use the high-pressure hoses at their discretion. The one drawback of self-service car washes is that the murderer can't wash the underside of the car. That is why the trained detective always notifies car washes in the immediate area as well as the owners of self-service car washes about the suspect. The investigators may even put surveillance teams at these locations, since many self-service car washes do not have people on the premises to look for vehicles matching the description of the murder vehicle.

Investigation and Capture

The examination of the suspected vehicle is done by detectives immediately upon receiving information that a vehicle may be the one in question. Vehicular homicide experts say that proper examination and evaluation of physical evidence are the keys to solving these types of murder. First investigators look for dents and scratches, which can be tricky since it's difficult to determine how recent the damage is and the exact cause of it. Clues of the victim's impact with the vehicle lead to further investigation by the detectives. They also check for broken parts because pieces of glass may remain in the headlight or may fall into the grill. A broken emblem or side mirror also attracts the detectives' attention.

A forensic analysis of the headlights or taillights can reveal if the lights were on or off at the point of impact. Filament structure and examination can determine whether or not the murder was committed with the vehicle's headlights on or off.

This is important in showing intent, and intent to kill is very important in the trial of a suspected murderer. If the lights were off, the suspect was probably attempting to run down the victim.

The trained gumshoes also look for fibers, since contact with the victim's clothing may leave fibers or even cloth on the vehicle. And if the vehicle struck the victim with sufficient force, an outline of the clothing pattern may be seen on the paint of the murderer's vehicle.

Other valuable evidence includes glass fragments from the headlights or sidelights and pieces from the vehicle's grill or hood ornament, which is usually found on a luxury vehicle. Additionally, metal fragments and paint flakes that may have fallen from the vehicle, tire impressions and other pieces of trim that may have been knocked off or may have fallen off (radio antenna, fender, trim, hubcaps) are useful in aiding the detectives in the capture of the murderer.

Trace evidence; the whereabouts, friendships, enemies and work habits of the victim; and forensic evidence at the scene lead the police to determine the victim's patterns. But as is true with other killings, the most important piece of evidence at the scene of a vehicular homicide is the body. So detectives focus on the victim and, in particular, the victim's clothing, which should be removed and studied for the following: grease from the understructure of the vehicle, tire marks, which may be irregular because of the yielding action of the clothing, and paint (the buttons and sometimes the cloth may retain paint from the car). Sometimes the victim's chest or back bears a distinct tire mark, a hood mark, an ornamental mark or an impression from the grill or bumper of the murderer's vehicle.

As mentioned earlier in the chapter, this type of murderer often borrows a vehicle from a friend or relative or rents one and reports it stolen shortly after the accident. It is also common for a vehicle to be stolen simply for the use of murdering someone. The vehicle, however, is usually stolen immediately prior to the intended use so as not to attract attention to it prior to the killing. Many a vehicular homicide suspect has been caught with a stolen vehicle days before the actual homicide, only to be arrested for grand larceny and not for the actual intended murder. Of course, through confessions and informants, we have learned that murder was the intended use of the vehicle, but the actual suspect can only be charged with receiving stolen property or grand larceny.

Case Study: A Bizarre Type of Vehicular Homicide

In one unusual case, the victim was not struck by the vehicle; she was actually seated inside it, right next to the murderer.

The scenario was as follows: A man was despondent over his wife's infidelity. Unable to forgive her, he wanted revenge for this betrayal. He wanted to kill her. But unlike some spouses who, after the murder, give themselves up or, worse, kill themselves, this husband did not want to get caught. He decided to make it appear as if he wanted to "patch things up," and in the course of doing so, he would murder her.

He asked his wife on a lovely spring day to go for a ride with him, and he said they'd take a picnic lunch they would pick up on the way. She reluctantly agreed, and after stopping at several stores, picking up food and supplies, the husband drove into the rolling hills of the countryside. Eventually his wife drifted off to sleep, and the man began looking for an opportunity to carry out his plan. The opportunity appeared in the form of a massive oak tree adjacent to the road near a sharp curve. After bypassing the curve several times slowly, he drove back to the main approach and made a soft U-turn on the dried dirt fields surrounding the farms in this area. Without stopping or braking, he built up speed until he reached the curve, whereupon he cut the wheel sharply to the left. The vehicle skidded off the road, and the passenger side of the vehicle slammed into the tree, instantly killing the suspect's wife.

When the state police authorities who had jurisdiction over this area arrived, they found the wife crushed to death in the vehicle and the husband mumbling incoherently beside her, still strapped in with his seat belt. The state police noticed that the wife did not have any seatbelt on and that she was thrown against her husband's body after the initial impact.

The husband was airlifted to a hospital where, several days later, he began to recover. He was interrogated by detectives who informed him that his wife was still alive and had given a written statement that she had observed him driving up and down the road, preparing to commit the murder by slamming into the tree. Faced with this crucial piece of factual "evidence," the husband gave a formal written confession to the detectives outlining the motives for the murder. The detectives had tricked him and had lied to him, but that is totally permissible in obtaining a truthful confession.

What had really occurred was that the detectives had located a witness tending a farm field who had observed the husband driving back and forth. The witness was an illegal alien and had reluctantly come forward, having to decide between possibly being deported to his native country or cooperating with the authorities to catch a murderer. The witness was actually given a hero's welcome by the mayor of the town, who, being so thankful for the man's cooperation, processed the paperwork for the farmhand to become a U.S. citizen.

This is a case of vehicular homicide where both the murderer and victim are present in the vehicle and the victim is murdered while in the vehicle instead of being struck by it. But remember: This is an extremely rare and relatively unheard-of type of vehicular homicide. We have spoken with detectives in many municipalities and have only heard of one or two other jurisdictions that have had similar types of murders. Of course, there may have been hundreds of vehicular accidents and deaths each year that were not properly investigated and that could have been this type of murder but, for one reason or another, were never determined to be so.

Other Vehicular Homicides

Automobiles are not the only weapons used in vehicular killings. We investigated a case of a hit-and-run homicide on water that involved several people in a small rowboat who had been killed when their boat was hit by a fast-moving speedboat that left the scene without being identified. Marks found on the speedboat contained the paint of the rowboat, and pieces of one of the victim's clothing were entwined in the propeller of the speedboat.

Both the operator and the passenger were subsequently convicted of vehicular homicide involving a vessel.

The motive of this homicide involved the victims' in the small rowboat yelling curses and giving the universal symbol of the middle finger to the speedboaters for the large wakes the boat was creating. The men in the speedboat responded by circling the rowboat and deliberately striking it, immediately killing both passengers.

BIZARRE MURDERS

Every once in a while, a homicide comes along that is so strange it does not fit any other pattern we've investigated before. These murders, which for the purpose of this chapter we will identify as bizarre murders, are committed by people from all walks of life and socioeconomic situations.

These bizarre murders do not fit the pattern of other murders for several reasons. It may be that the manner in which the victim was killed does not involve methods or weapons, or it may also be that normal weapons were used but to a different degree or to a certain extreme. Usually these bizarre murders involve rituals, voodoo or extreme degradation of the human body during the murder.

Ritual Murders

The term "ritual murder" implies the taking of a human life for religious purposes in accordance with a religious or magic rite. The term was used to describe a type of murder that became a serious problem in Basutoland, South Africa, in 1947 and 1948. At that time, the British government appointed G. Jones, a lecturer in anthropology at the University of Cambridge, to inquire into the nature and causes of these ritual murders. His investigation revealed that the people of Basutoland were killing other people within their families and exchanging the flesh and blood with their own to keep themselves young or were carving out poisons thought to be detriments to the human body, thus making the body pure.

These types of ritualistic murders usually follow a regular pattern. They are always premeditated and are committed by a group of people for a specific purpose, for example, removing the bad part of the victim's body while he is still alive to improve the body.

In one case we investigated, strips of flesh were removed from the victim and eaten by other members of the family for the betterment of the unit. The family in this investigation was not strictly the blood family but a group of people, including the family of the victim, that had bonded together for the purpose of ritualistic murders. These murders were not committed out of any anger or hate toward the victims; they simply felt that eating the flesh of the victims—who were much younger and in better strength—would enable them to live longer. They believed that the body died and decomposed from the lack of fresh and pure flesh. When any one of them had erred or sinned in any way, they felt their flesh was no longer satisfactory for other members of the family and they had to move on to outside people. Eventually, strangers were being killed for their strips of flesh, which were actually peeled off the victims while they were alive, using scalpels and straight razors. These killings almost always occurred on sandy beaches with small fires for burning incense, which seemed to exhilarate the murderers as they were performing their rituals.

Voodoo Murders

In another bizarre murder, called voodoo murder, the killers are sorcerers who use black magic and other such practices to murder a person who has been the cause of an offense. Voodoo death has been reported from the island of Haiti, Africa, Australia and other countries. It has been suggested that poisons have been used to murder the victims, who have no idea they are being killed. While this may be true in some cases, we've investigated many cases of death occurring as a direct result of voodoo rituals in which the victims were murdered and often dismembered and the killers wanted the victims to know what was being done against them and to fear it.

Case Study: Voodoo Killing

An officer on a routine early-morning patrol of a seashore community stumbled upon a group of people engaging in a voodoo murder under an elevated wooden boardwalk. The officer heard chanting and groaning under the boardwalk and thought it was just the customary late-night couples engaging in a little bit of sexual pleasure. Upon trying to ascertain exactly what was down there, he stumbled on a person who was dressed in full witch doctor regalia and pointing a human bone at another individual.

A large group of people humming and chanting indiscernible phrases and music encircled the two. According to the officer, the person at whom the bone was being pointed stood with his hands lifted as though to ward off a blow from a lethal instrument. His cheeks were extremely white, his eyes were glassy and wide with fear and his face was horribly contorted and twisted. The victim shrieked and began to tremble, his muscles twitching involuntarily as if he were having some type of attack. He shortly fell backward to the ground and, after a small period of time, appeared to be swimming. Then he began twitching on the ground as if he was in agonizing mortal pain, covering his face with his hands and moaning uncontrollably.

At this point, the officer saw what would be his final observation before he, too, became violently ill. Then the person immediately jumped to his feet and began vomiting into a large metal bucket. As the police officer watched in disbelief, all the members of the group dipped their hands into this bucket and actually drank and chewed the vomit from the person that was being placed under this "spell."

While this officer was clutching his own stomach and

attempting not to vomit, he observed the final suffering of the victim. The person pointing the bone—apparently the witch doctor—walked over to this groaning individual, doused him with a liquid and immediately set a match to him. The victim screamed in agony, running around under the boardwalk completely immersed in flames.

There was nothing the police officer could do but attempt to arrest the witch doctor, since he had been the one to set fire to the victim. The officer moved in and identified himself by screaming that he was the police and telling everyone not to move. The members of the circle then attacked him and began biting him all over different parts of his body. After this prolonged attack, his assailants left the scene, leaving the officer in a pile of burned ash, bones and flesh.

This officer endured mental trauma so severe that he had to be removed from the police department on a medical disability. According to his closest friends, he frequently awakens in the middle of the night screaming and, on many occasions, has attempted suicide. It is believed that the trauma of watching the voodoo murder made him this way, and frequent psychological evaluations confirm that he is suffering from extreme and prolonged trauma. Unfortunately, the murder victim was never identified and neither were any of the participants in the killing.

Links Between Cannibalism, Voodoo Murders and Ritualistic Murders

Cannibalism, voodoo murder and ritualistic murder seem inherently linked. The flesh and blood of the dead are commonly eaten and drunk to inspire bravery, wisdom or other remarkable qualities the victim once had. These qualities are believed to be located in particular parts of the body.

In the mountain tribes of southeastern Africa, there are sects in which youths are formed into guilds or lodges, and one of the rights of initiation is intended to infuse courage, intelligence and other qualities into these novices. Whenever an enemy who has behaved with conspicuous bravery is killed, his liver (considered the seat of valor), his ears (the supposed seat of intelligence), the skin of his forehead (the seat of perseverance), his testicles (the seat of strength) and his arms and legs (the seat of various other virtues) are cut from his body and baked to cinders. The ashes are carefully kept in a bull's horn and during ceremonies are mixed with other ingredients into a kind of paste that is then administered by the tribal priest to the youth. This paste symbolizes all the virtues of the victim, which are believed to be imparted to the eaters.

Modern-Day Bizarre Murders

Cannibalism

There are various motives of cannibalism in modern-day bizarre murders. We all know about Jeffrey Dahmer and his propensity for eating human flesh. He achieved a kind of sexual gratification by doing so, which is not uncommon in bizarre murders where cannibalism is present.

Case Study: Albert Fish

In 1928, a New York couple permitted a casual friend to take their ten-year-old daughter to a children's party. The young girl was never seen again, and all efforts to trace her abductor failed. In 1934, the mother received an unsigned letter in the mail addressed to her. In this letter, the person wrote her that he had been told by a friend of his, who was a deckhand on a steamer in China, about the famine that had occurred there in 1894. He wrote that, according to his friend, the suffering was so great among the poor that children under twelve years old were sold to butchers to be cut up for food in order to keep others from starving. According to this letter writer, his friend had told him that, while in China, a boy or girl under fourteen was not safe on the street. And he wrote that you could go in any shop and ask for steak, chops or stew meat, at which point, parts of a naked body of a boy or girl would be brought out and whatever you wanted was cut from it. A boy or girl's behind, which was considered in China at that time to be the sweetest part of the body, was sold as veal cutlets and commanded the highest price.

In this letter, the bizarre murderer stated that his friend had also told him that once he had arrived in New York, he stole two boys, one seven and one eleven. He took them to his home, stripped them naked, tied them in a closet and burned everything they had on. According to this letter writer, his friend spanked them several times a day and at night, torturing them to make their meat good and tender. Finally, he killed the eleven-year-old boy because he had the fattest behind with, of course, the most meat on it. His friend then said that he cooked the boy's body and ate everything except the head, bone and guts, which he had roasted in the oven. All of his behind was broiled, fried and stewed. The littler boy was next, and he went the same way.

The bizarre murderer finally informed the New York mother about the murder of her daughter. The killer had gone to visit the woman and her family and brought her some fresh fruit. During the time he was there, the victim's mother gave him lunch while the little girl sat on his lap and gave him a kiss. He stated in his letter that he made up his mind at that exact point in time to eat her and would do so on the pretext of taking her to the party. Once he got the mother's permission, he took the girl to an empty home in Westchester that he had already picked out. He wrote that when he got there, he asked the girl to remain outside. While she picked flowers, he went upstairs and took off all of his clothes off so he would not get her blood on them. When he was all ready, he went to the window and called her in. He then hid in the closet until the girl was in the room. When he came out, she saw he was naked and began to cry and tried to run downstairs. The bizarre murderer wrote that he then grabbed her and she said she would tell her mother. Then he stripped her naked and she kicked and bit him. Finally, he wrote, he choked her to death and cut her into small pieces so he could take the meat to his room, which was in a boarding-house, and cook it and eat it. He went on to tell the victim's mother that the girl's sweet and tender little behind was roasted in his oven. It took him nine days, he stated, to eat her entire body. He said he did not have intercourse with her although he could have; she died a virgin, which was the sweetest meat he could possibly eat.

Although the letter was unsigned, the police succeeded in finding the writer, Albert Fish, who was a sixty-five-year-old housepainter and the father of six children. He confessed that he had strangled the girl and dismembered her body. He went on to tell the police that he took parts of her body home with him, cooked them in various ways with carrots, onion and strips of bacon and ate them over a period of nine days. During all this time, he was in a state of sexual excitement. He ate the flesh during the day and thought about it during the night. He spoke in a matter-of-fact way, almost like a homemaker describing her favorite methods of cooking. His previous criminal record included arrests for grand larceny, bad checks and sending obscene letters through the mail. He had been admitted to several mental hospitals, only to be released within in a short time on each occasion. However, it was clear he was suffering from a paranoid psychosis.

Upon being analyzed by psychologists, Fish told them that for years he had been sticking needles into his body in his genital area between the rectum and the scrotum. They were needles of assorted sizes, some of them big and some small. He also told police he had done this to other people, too—especially to children. At first, he said, he only stuck these needles into himself a short distance and then pulled them out again. Others he had stuck in so far he wasn't able to get them out and they stayed there. Upon being arrested, he informed the detectives that the needles were in there right now, and when asked how many, he said he didn't know. A series of X-rays and pelvic and abdominal region examinations revealed twenty-nine needles inside his body, twenty-seven of which were in his pelvic region. In some instances, the eyes of the needles were clear. Some of them were eroded to such an extent they must have been there at least seven years. Some were so deeply embedded they were in rather dangerous places, including some just above and beside the transverse and descending colon, several fragments around the rectum and others in the bladder region. These X-rays are unique in the history of medical science.

Fish's explanation for murder was that he had visions of Christ and his angels and saw Christ mumbling words Fish couldn't understand. Sometimes, he was sure the voices he heard came from visions and angels. Other times, he didn't know where the voices came from, but he heard them saying words like *stripes*, *rewardeth* and *delighteth*. He connected these words with the Bible and elaborated upon their meanings to fit his own sadistic wishes. He interpreted *stripes* to mean that he should lash his victims, for example.

In his statement, Fish said he felt driven to torment and kill children. He wanted to offer the children as sacrifices to purge himself of his sins and abnormalities in the eyes of God. Sometimes, he said, he would gag them, tie them up and beat them—although he preferred not to gag them because he liked to hear their cries. Fish also said he was ordered by God to castrate little boys.

The estimate of the number of children Fish murdered varies from five to eighteen. At the trial for the murder of the victim he mentioned in the letter, his plea of insanity was rejected and he was sentenced to death by electrocution.

The most ironic twist in this whole case was that when Fish's little victim noticed he had left the package containing his knife, saw and cleaver on the train on which they'd been traveling, she hurried back and brought it to him. With these tools, she was later dismembered by Fish.

Delusional Killers

Another bizarre murder we have personally investigated involved a young woman addicted to crack cocaine who enjoyed having sex with numerous men in the neighborhood where she rented an apartment. Neighbors frequently complained about the constant parade of men going in and out of the apartment at all times of the day and night. On one occasion, the woman, while having sexual intercourse with a casual friend, had delusions and psychotic fantasies that the man's penis was actually a snake that was going in and out of her. She immediately pulled away and started screaming but would not divulge her fears to the man, who subsequently fell asleep.

The woman, however, remained awake and delusional, deciding she must kill the snake. She remembered seeing on television that a large bolt cutter was frequently used to snip off the head of a snake, thereby rendering it immobile and unable to bite a victim. So she stumbled into her garage where several tools had been left by handymen, with whom she had also engaged in sexual intercourse over the course of years. Armed with a bolt cutter, she proceeded to the sleeping victim and snipped off his penis with one blow. The man, upon awakening in agony, screamed, but he had lost so much blood he could not escape. The woman kept at the genital area with the bolt cutter and eventually succeeded in snipping off his testicles, as well as tearing up both sides of his thighs.

Had it not been for our noticing the bolt cutter, we would have thought he had been shot with a shotgun in the genital area because of the many gorges and open, gaping wounds. Upon interviewing the neighbors, we discovered neighbors a full three blocks away who had heard the bloodcurdling screams.

The Ultimate Revenge

Another case we investigated involved a man who was extremely upset with his spouse, whom he believed was having an affair. He decided to exact the ultimate revenge upon his wife, who was a chef in a local restaurant. He subdued her one evening with an ammonia-soaked rag, then placed her in a double-wall oven and proceeded to bake her. The neighbors called the police when they smelled an extremely sour odor that was emanating from the victim's home. The police and the local authorities in the county found the murderer sitting in a chair, laughing hysterically. He obviously was suffering from some type of delusional psychosis, but was absolutely ecstatic he had exacted this revenge upon his wife in the manner he had.

It was later discovered that the wife's suspicious trips were not to her boyfriend's home, as the husband had thought, but to a second part-time job. She had told her friends she was secretly working the second job in order to save up money for a new set of golf clubs her husband wanted for his birthday. And it was the husband's delusions of her infidelity that led him to kill her!

Summary

As you can see, bizarre murders are so extremely contrary to human nature they just do not fit the mold of any other pattern of murder. That Jeffrey Dahmer killed many people and cut up their bodies isn't outside our realm of belief. But the fact that

Dahmer dissected these corpses and ate them is beyond our wildest dreams.

Just how bizarre "bizarre murders" will be twenty, thirty or forty years from now depends on the state of society in general. Murders that occurred in the 1950s and 1960s were shocking at the time, but now, thanks to increasingly violent movies and television shows, we've become somewhat inured to all but the most deviant of crimes. Similarly, what seems bizarre today will not likely be bizarre twenty years from now.

Bizarre murderers can come from all walks of life. This type of killer may be rich or poor, an imbecile or a genius. And the manner of the murder will be as bizarre as the murderer's rationale for committing it.

Glossary

ANNIVERSARY REACTION—Behavior exhibited by an individual on an anniversary of a traumatic event.

AUTOEROTIC FATALITY—Death that occurs during solo-sexual activities. Such deaths are accidental and most often involve hanging.

COMFORT ZONE—Geographical area with which an offender is familiar and relaxed. It is normally within walking distance (1½) miles of where the criminal lives, works or regularly frequents.

CONCEALED—Method of disposing of the body after death. This term refers to those instances in which the killer made a concerted effort to ensure the body would not be found or to delay discovery. This method is most commonly used by the "organized" killer.

CORE BEHAVIOR—Three forms of behavior that are fantasy driven and demonstrate the motivation for a sexual assault. The behaviors are verbal (what offender says or demands victim say), physical (intentional injurious force used during sexual assault) and sexual (type and sequence of sexual acts in which a victim is forced to participate).

CRIMINAL INVESTIGATIVE ANALYSIS—Term used to describe the various investigative support services (other than VICAP) provided by the NCAVC. Included services are Indirect Personality Assessment, Equivocal Death Analysis, Investigative Suggestions, Trial Strategy, Characteristics and Traits (profile) of Unidentified Offenders, Interview Strategy and Threat Assessment.

DISORGANIZED CRIME—Crime that was committed in an impulsive manner with little or no planning preceding it. The crime exhibits a lack of offender control over the victim and/or self.

DISPLAYED—Method of disposing the body after death. This term refers to those instances in which the killer places the body in a location where it is certain to be discovered. He may also position the body in such a way as to degrade the victim (e.g., legs widely spread), to protect the dignity of the victim (e.g., redressing the body or covering it) or to shock society or the individuals finding the body. Generally, this method is used by the "organized" killer.

DISPOSAL SITE—Location where the killer left the victim's body. It may or may not be the death scene. In serial murder cases, the killer may use one or more disposal sites for a series of victims.

DUMPED—Method of disposing the body after death. This term refers to those instances in which the killer made little or no effort to conceal the body. Haste is the killer's primary objective when this method is utilized. This method is most commonly used by the "disorganized" murderer.

EQUIVOCAL DEATH—Death in which the manner of death (homicide, suicide, accident) is still undetermined after a complete criminal and medicolegal investigation.

EROTICA—Item that is sexually stimulating to an individual. One is cautioned not to apply one's own arousal patterns when looking for such materials. While pornography is a common form of erotica, nonpornographic literature or objects may be erotic to a given individual.

FEMININE TOUCH—Term used to describe an activity that is commonly associated with the female gender (e.g., baking a cake, cleaning the house, washing/ironing clothes, going to the beauty parlor). Many women who commit suicide engage in such behavior prior to killing themselves.

HIGH-RISK CRIME—Crime committed at a time or location that posed a great threat of discovery to the offender. This category of crime is normally attributed to the "disorganized" criminal personality. Use of alcohol or other drugs greatly enhances the risk potential of the offender by lowering that person's inhibitions.

HIGH-RISK VICTIM—Person who because of occupation, sexual history, lifestyle or a given set of circumstances is highly vulnerable to a violent crime. Such victims make the crime analysis a very difficult undertaking.

INDIRECT PERSONALITY ASSESSMENT—Formerly referred to as "personality assessment." Assessment of a known individual believed to be responsible for the commission of a violent crime. This technique is utilized in preparing for cross-examination during trial, interviews and interrogations, equivocal deaths and other similar situations.

INVESTIGATIVE SUGGESTIONS—Formally referred to as "proactive techniques." Techniques designed to influence offender behavior and cause predictive actions on the criminal's part.

LINKAGE ANALYSIS—Linkage of a series of crimes via the behavior (MO and ritual) of the offender.

LOW-RISK CRIME—Crime committed at a time or location that posed little or no risk to the offender. This category of crime is typically associated with the "organized" criminal personality.

LOW-RISK VICTIM—Person whose victimology (sexual habits, lifestyle, pastimes, etc.) contains no information to suggest the person would become the victim of a violent attack. In such instances, one can begin with the hypothesis that the offender either specifically targeted the victim, took advantage of the vulnerability of the person or was personally associated with the individual.

LUST MURDER—Murders that involve the postmortem mutilation and/or removal of the sexual areas of the body. The mutilation must have been intentionally inflicted after death. Such crimes are generally carried out by the "disorganized" offender.

MIXED—Combination of the "organized" and "disorganized" characteristics. The crime may appear to be "mixed" due to two offenders being present, the youthfulness of the offender, the involvement of alcohol or other drugs, mental illness or a lack of criminal sophistication on the part of the offender.

MO—Method of operation, or modus operandi, of a given criminal. MO is learned behavior that is ever changing. It is developed over a period of time and its principle functions are to protect the offender's security and safety, ensure success and facilitate escape.

MODERATE-RISK VICTIM—Person who is not normally expected to become the victim of a violent crime, but because of the environment or what the individual is doing at the time of confrontation, the risk of becoming a victim of a violent attack is elevated.

NUISANCE SEXUAL OFFENSE—Nonfelony sexual crimes, such as window peeping (Peeping Tom), exhibitionism (flashing), telephone scatology (obscene phone calls), writing obscene notes and frottage (rubbing against another).

ONE NEAT AND CONTROLLED ASPECT—Feature of the "disorganized" crime (having nothing to do with the body or sex) that is inconsistent with a "disorganized" offense. It is completely out of sync with all other features of the crime. For example, a victim who was eviscerated with a weapon from her residence is found in her blood-splattered room. Blood is found on the walls, doors, ceiling and floor, but no blood is on the baseboards of the room. The killer had taken a towel from the closet, wiped the baseboards and replaced the towel in the closet. The presence of such an anomaly indicates the involvement of an individual who has been released from a mental institution within the past four to six months.

ORGANIZED CRIME—Crime exhibiting a great deal of thought and planning. The offender has maintained control over the victim(s) and self. Few or no items of evidentiary value are present. The crime was carried out in a criminally sophisticated and methodical manner.

OVERKILL—Victim's body exhibits much more trauma than was necessary to end life. Such a feature indicates personalized anger and suggests the offender knew the victim.

PARAPHILIA—Formerly termed "sexual deviation." Behavior characterized by intense sexual acts or fantasies generally involving (1) inanimate objects and/or (2) suffering or humiliation of self or another and/or (3) children or other nonconsenting partners. The behavior may or may not be harmful to the individual or others. The most common paraphilias are exhibitionism, fetishism, frotteurism, pedophilia, sexual masochism, sexual sadism, transvestic-fetishism and voyeurism.

PARAPHILIAC—One who demonstrates a paraphilia.

PIQUERISM—Psychiatric term used to describe a sexual arousal pattern derived from the piercing of the body with a pointed instrument. A piquer has a history of using needles, or other sharp objects, against women in public locations (e.g., store, bus, elevator).

POSTOFFENSIVE BEHAVIOR—Behavior of the subject within hours, days and weeks following the crime. When described by the analyst, such behavior distinguishes the offender from the rest of the suspect population.

PREOFFENSE BEHAVIOR—Behavior of the offender just prior to committing a crime. Often, a precipitate stressor is the catalyst for the commission of a violent crime.

PRIMARY FACTOR—Feature of the crime that directly relates to a characteristic/trait of an offender. For example, one neat or controlled aspect suggests that the unidentified offender has been in a mental institution and released within the past four to six months.

PROFILE—Term commonly used to describe the written or verbal results of an investigative analysis of an unsolved crime of violence. A profile may include all of the following sections: Victimology, Crime Reconstruction, Behaviorally Significant Facts of the Autopsy, Characteristics and Traits of the Offender, Postoffense Behavior and Investigative Suggestions.

PROPRIETARY INTEREST—Material interest in a physical item because of ownership by the offender. In violent crimes, analysts sometimes note that precautions were taken to protect something owned by, and of value to, the offender (e.g., a man kills his wife, places the body in her car, drives it to an airport parking lot and locks the doors, taking the keys with him). Most often, this feature is observed in "staged" scenes.

RITUAL—Repetitive and psychosexually gratifying behavior of a sexual offender. This is not to be confused with the modus operandi or method of operation (MO).

SECONDARY FACTOR—Characteristic of the offender derived not from the crime but from a "primary factor." For example, if the primary factor was mental institutionalization, a secondary factor would be that the offender is unlikely to have a driver's license.

SEXUAL BONDAGE—Physical and/or emotional binding or self (masochistic) or another (sadistic) for sexual excitement. It may be demonstrated by restriction of the senses (e.g., blinds, gags, hoods) or by the restriction of movement of the limbs. Sexual bondage is manifested by one or more of these four characteristics: symmetry, unnecessary bindings, variety of positions, extreme care in the placement of the bindings (neatness).

SEXUAL RITUALISM—Acts committed by the offender that are unnecessary to the accomplishment of the crime. Such acts are repeated by the offender over a series of crimes. The acts are performed to increase the killer's psychosexual gratification. Ritualism must not be confused with modus operandi.

SOUVENIR—Personal item belonging to the victim of a violent crime that is taken by the offender. Item most commonly taken: an article of jewelry or clothing, photograph or driver's license. The item taken from the victim is a reminder of a pleasurable encounter and may be used for masturbatory fantasies. The offender taking an item as a souvenir is typically an inadequate person who is likely to keep it for a long period of time or give it away to a significant other. (Please refer to "Trophy.")

STAGED SCENE—Crime scene in which someone (most often the offender) arranges the scene or commits certain acts to have the scene convey a motivational intent different from the original motive or to mislead investigators as to the logical suspect.

THREAT ASSESSMENT—Analysis of written or verbal communications that contain direct or implied threats to perpetuate harm or injury to individuals, industry, institutions or governmental agencies. The communication is analyzed for content and stylistic characteristics, and the analysis may include a profile of the unknown author/caller. The analysis may also include an evaluation of the potential for the unknown subject to carry out the threat.

THRESHOLD DIAGNOSIS—A term used to describe an impulsively-provided opinion about a case without having access to all pertinent facts, or prior to having analyzed available case materials.

TRIAL STRATEGY—Assistance rendered to prosecuting attorneys in the planning or conduct of a criminal trial. Such assistance may involve "Indirect Personality Assessment" and may include preparing the attorneys for cross-examination of subjects or expert witnesses, suggestions for opening or closing remarks to the jury, or assisting the prosecutor by being present during the conduct of the trial.

TROPHY—A personal item belonging to the victim of a violent crime which is taken by the responsible offender. Most commonly taken items include: an article of jewelry or clothing, a drivers' license or a photograph. The item represents a victory or conquest to the criminal and may be used for masturbatory fantasies. The offender who takes a "trophy" is typically an aggressive individual who is unlikely to retain the item and may dispose of it or give it to a significant other in his life. (Please refer to "Souvenir.")

UNDOING—An attempt by the killer to symbolically undo the act. For example, a man stabbed his victim 52 times, then washed the body and placed band-aids over each of the wounds.

VICAP—An acronym for Violent Crime Apprehension Program.

VICTIMOLOGY—The history of a victim which impacts on the analysis of the crime. Such history would include personality characteristics, strengths and weaknesses, occupation, hobbies, life-style and sexual history.

Index